# Foot Notes

# FOOT NOTES

## GUY KENNAWAY AND HUSSEIN SHARIF

MENSCH PUBLISHING

Mensch Publishing
51 Northchurch Road, London N1 4EE, United Kingdom

First published in Great Britain 2021

A catalogue record for this book is available from the British Library

ISBN: HB: 978-1-912914-26-5; eBook: 978-1-912914-27-2

2 4 6 8 10 9 7 5 3 1

Typeset by Newgen KnowledgeWorks Pvt. Ltd., Chennai, India
Printed and bound in Great Britain by CPI Group (UK) Ltd, Croydon CR0 4YY

This book is dedicated to my grandchildren, Ezra, Lola, Nahla, Amour, and the one soon to be born.

*That's just the way it is,*
*Things will never be the same.*

This book describes events which occurred between 2018 and 2020. Hussein and Guy are our real names, but some of the other people in the book have had their names changed to protect their privacy.

# 1.

Without making it obvious, I double-checked my car was locked and glanced through the side window to see if there were valuables in view. I saw just two books on the back seat, objects unlikely to be the targets of any thieves on St Albans Road, Tottenham, London NE17. Only a couple of days earlier, someone had been the victim of knife crime, as they daintily called being stabbed to death, on its food-splattered tarmac. I doubted it was a fight about books. A hoodied youth on a bike turned lingering circles on the cracked pavement, as though toying with me, and when I crossed the road pretending not to be avoiding him, though I was, I was casually monitored by some Rastas leaning against a wall next to a car with its bonnet up. I gave them all my I-am-firm-and-no-nonsense-but-definitely-not-racist smile.

It's necessary here to describe myself. I think I resemble mid-late James Coburn. Which is why it's always a bit dismaying to look in the mirror and see Benny Hill staring back. Yes. I am a slightly deluded pink, portly Englishman in his sixties, with thick grey hair and grey eyes. I say English, but actually I am mixed heritage – my father was indigenous Scottish, and my mother was born in Watford. You can't get much whiter than me.

After a week of sunbathing on holiday I do change colour, from flat white to magnolia, and then back to flat white when I'm on the plane home.

I was in Tottenham that October afternoon to pick up my new friend, Hussein, and introduce him to the British countryside. We were now related because his sister had given birth to my son's first child. At a family event we had found ourselves sitting next to each other at the lunch table and I said to him, 'I've never met anyone like you. A young Muslim living in an inner-city council flat. I've seen you depicted in movies and you're always on the TV news, often throwing something at the police, but I've never actually met anyone like you.'

He said, 'I've never met anyone like you. I've seen your type – white, middle age, middle class and male, in loads of films and you're always on TV, usually the Police Commissioner in charge of the cops being pelted with rocks, but I've never met anyone like you in my life.'

We discovered we had one thing, at least, in common: a high level of anxiety. I told him that when life got too stressful to me, I calmed my jitters by taking a long walk and somehow, from there, we hatched a plan to go on foot across Britain together.

I planned a forty-mile hike along the Offa's Dyke Path, up the English/Welsh border, a rich stretch of undulating landscape where I could show Hussein the splendour of the country, and explain to him the many delights of our historic culture, as this was the county of Elgar and Housman and not far from the birthplace of William Shakespeare. That way, I argued, he would feel more excited about being British than he seemed thus far to be, cooped up and a bit pissed off in a small apartment in Tottenham. Fresh air, fine landscape, and frank exchanges on a walk through the Shropshire hills would soon show him how lucky he was to have made a life in the UK. I would hum Elgar and declaim Housman. Which reminded me, I needed to look up Housman as I had forgotten it all. My chosen route went between two friends who had farms on the footpath, forty miles apart. The first lived in a Georgian mansion, the second in an Elizabethan house, both of which struck historical notes which I particularly wanted Hussein to appreciate.

I am aware I am controlling this narrative.

And I know my hands are heavy on its steering wheel.

I am also aware that telling these kinds of narratives is exactly what my type of person has been doing to Hussein's type – can I even say that? – for ... for millennia. Is that long enough? At least in Europe. I am holding some people down, and holding them back, with my words.

But I want to change. I want to see it another way. I am, frankly, bored of my own perspective – after all, most books, films, plays, songs, you name it, are written from it and, unlike those who believe in identity politics, I think I am quite capable of seeing things another way. Hussein's way, for instance. I wrote an entire novel from the point of view of a pheasant (*Bird Brain*, read it), so I reckon I can get my head around a fellow human being living a different experience. For me, identity politics is a gateway drug to full blown racism.

But I needed a de-colonisation of my narrative.

That sounds like a medical procedure. Bend over, Guy, this is going to hurt.

But how could I jump the rails of my white male privilege, and see things a different way?

I guess I had to hear Hussein's own words, in his own voice. And I could only do that by asking him his opinion. But even if I asked for his version of events, and wrote them into this book, I would still be the author of his words. I would still be in control. The narrative would still be colonised.

The best solution I can come up with is to allow Hussein to have his own say, without interpretation from me. To correct my mistakes, and to dispute or corroborate my observations as he sees fit. That way he can create his own reality, and show me who he is, as I show him who I am. I have therefore decided to allow him to make a commentary on my text. Say fifty words at the end of each chapter.[1]

All right, Hussein, you chime in whenever you want, on any page, in the footnotes.

Hussein was born in Somalia, grew up in Kenya and arrived in London when he was eight years old. [2] He was now twenty-one, and had recently dropped out of Canterbury University[3] suffering from anxiety so acute it kept him pinned down at home. He had difficulty going on public transport, so I had driven the round

[1]No deal. That's like being set homework.
[2]Salam. This is Hussein here. I'm trying out being in Guy's little box at the bottom of his page where he has put me in his attempt to woke his book. I was actually born in Kenya, on the Swahili coast, and grew up in London. Not a good start, Guy.
[3]I went to Kent University, thirty-seven places above Canterbury on the league table.

4

trip of seven hours from my place in Somerset to pick him up.[4]

Hussein lived with his sister, her kids, his mum, his aunt, and three of his younger brothers in a flat on an estate not far from the White Hart Lane stadium in Tottenham.

The Victorian terraced street, which I was now walking down towards Hussein's block reminded me of Notting Hill in the late 70s. Apart from some Windrush-esque splashes of exterior gloss it was fairly run down. There were not yet any new sash windows, plantation shutters or Farrow and Balled front doors, but a mattress and some rubble in one front garden was a sign that someone was upgrading, and that this street in Tottenham was soon going to be colonised by tribes of gentrifyers pushing north through Highbury.

The council estate I was heading for was gentrification-proof. As was standard for 1960s public housing, it had slow and ugly decline designed into it. When I first visited my new family, I had felt intimidated going there. I had never set foot in a council flat in all my life. Actually, that was not quite true: I had twice entered council flats and both were owned by someone well off who was trying to scam the council either into selling it, or subletting it for profit. I had definitely never visited someone living on a council estate like this one.

I know. That says something about me, and it's not altogether good, is it?

[4] I suffer from panic attacks. My first proper panic attack happened in a taxi on the last day of uni on my way back home to London, I don't know why. The anxiety tends to disappear when I'm outside London.

When I had first visited the housing estate, two years earlier, I had been anxious about being held up at knife point for my phone. Good luck to them finding that. I had a coat over a tweed jacket and a gilet; even when it was ringing it took me about ten minutes to locate it. I diverted myself from my anxiety imagining a world in which people were mugged for books (*"Mi 'ave gun. Mi wan 'ardback"*).

Much to my surprise, there seemed to be something familiar about the uneven paving, rank alleyways and scrofulous grass between the tower blocks. Then I realised it was in the landscape of the TV shows of my youth. In a flat on the sixth floor of that block over there, Rodney was being bollocked by Del Boy, while their three-wheeler stood parked by the boarded-up shops. Arthur Daly's Jag was safe in his railway arch over there and Arthur was filling Terry in on a scam in that dilapidated pub on the corner. The only confusing thing was that Dennis Waterman was also careering down this street in a squad car chasing a villain who was making for the locks-up round the back, the place the robbers always seemed to head for in The Sweeney.[5]

I wondered if the people on the street thought I was a copper. The kind played by John Thaw. D.I. Regan, that was his name. Tough, grisled and with no sympathy for the underdog.

While I waited for Hussein to answer the intercom at the newly installed security door, I perused a notice board advertising the ward councillors. The intercom

[5]If you don't understand Guy's TV and movie references, don't worry I have no idea too. I mean, how old is he?

was surprisingly serviceable; I could hear Hussein, and he me. The lock had not been tampered with and inside the building it was clean and tidy,[6] though the steel doors of the lift bore scratches where graffiti had been scoured off.

Waiting for the lift, I lost myself in my book-mugger game.

*Through a metal grille on a window off the walkway I glimpsed a filthy print den. Five bodies lay on the floor, one or two tragically young, holding out ten-pound notes, while a dealer went around them dishing out pages ripped from a novel. (Careful with this. It's strong. What's it? Burroughs. Burroughs? That's killer shit man. Yeah,* The Wild Boys. *American edition.)*

I can't help noticing that one of my little fantasies about the area featured violence, and the other drugs. That is called, I believe, textbook racism. Why do I have these thoughts? With that gloomy observation on my mind, I arrived at the flat.

Hussein answered the door, smiled anxiously, and turned away, leading me inside. He had a fuzz of wiry black hair, almost like an afro[7], a wispy beard, a hooked nose[8] that widened at the nostrils, and a look in his eyes that somehow combined panic and kindness. His skin was black. He was a black man, like I was a white man: extremely so. To a very high degree. If they ever do, as Blue Mink suggested in their 1969 hit, put a great big melting pot on the hob to turn out coffee-coloured

---

[6]Luckily you didn't use the back entrance which is usually covered with piss.
[7]It is an afro.
[8]Don't get me started on you.

people by the score, Hussein and I will be headed into the pot rather than being poured out onto the baking tray.[9] [10]

He's right. Installing Hussein at the bottom of the page in a diminutive font size has not solved the problem.

I have an American friend[11] who was an academic at the University in Kingston Jamaica whom I trusted on these kind of matters, so I asked her what she thought of giving Hussein footnotes.[12]

She said, 'I get where you are coming from, and I think it is interesting, but how comfortable are you with footnotes? I mean, I can see what you are trying to do, okay, but I remember in history at school being taught exclusively white stuff like the kings and queens of England, and then we would turn a page in the

[9] A few months after writing that sentence, I read an old piece from the *Times* (28/8/19) reporting that the song Melting Pot by Blue Mink had been withdrawn from radio playlists because of the racial language. Ofcom ruled it was offensive, despite the song being a wonderful if a little clumsy attempt to promote racial inclusivity and equality. As you have probably guessed, I don't mind clumsy, if the heart is true. The track is nostalgically offensive in a sweet way, not quite at the level of Guy Gibson level of offence. Plus, it's catchy.

[10] Hey, what are you doing down here bro? This is my little spot of the book. You said it was mine. You're even invading my footnotes. Talk about entitlement and privilege. Go back to where you came from. Up the top of the page.

[11] Katie Dieter, now at Stanford. Attend her lectures if you can, she's wise on race and gender.

[12] I don't care what Guy's friend the professor says. I'm done with being in a box at the bottom of his page.

textbook and, in a different colour with a box round it would be something about a Native Indian or slavery. That was our bit, reduced to that. You see?'

'Mmm,' I said. It was slightly annoying, since I had thought it solved my patriarchal narrative problem with Hussein.

'You might have to come up with another idea.'

'Mmm,' I said again.

'It might be a bit more complicated than you thought,' she laughed.

She was right. I was now feeling uncomfortable about the whole footnote idea. I liked the pun on walking. But by their very nature, footnotes are secondary to the main text, so I remained in the controlling position. I need to change the rules of the book so Hussein can be heard more.

I came up with a new idea: I will allow Hussein into the main text, but his words will appear in another colour, so our voices can be easily distinguished. I rang him to tell him about the plan. But first I spoke to Miranda, the editor of this book.[13]

'I was thinking of getting round the footnote problem by putting Hussein's remarks in red. It's a good idea, eh? Then our voices will have equal weight on the layout.'

'I'm afraid not, Guy,' said Miranda. 'A second colour is out of the question.'

'That's ironic.'

'It's cost. Charkin[14] won't pay for it.'

---

[13]Miranda Vaughan Jones, a talented and diligent editor, who is so tolerant of writers missing deadlines.

[14]Richard Charkin, owner of Mensch Publishing. A brilliant man with excellent taste.

'I'll have another think.'

'Hussein,' I said, when I finally tracked him down. He hadn't made it easy to get his number, I noticed. 'I want to talk to you about this footnotes idea.'

'Hold on, I'll just leave the room.' The shouts and shrieks of kids at play diminished.

Yuh? What?' He said.

'I wanted to let you write all over the book, not just in footnotes, but they won't let me use red, so we can see it's your voice.'

'Can I use emoticons, bro?'

'No. I hate them. You have to use words. This is a book not a teenage text message.'

'Not just teenagers use 'em, Guy. I fink you're getting left behind here.'

'You are not using emoticons, and Miranda has nixed a new font. I'm not sure why. I was thinking of putting you in brackets.'

'Wha?'

'No, you're right, you don't want to be bracketed.'

'Yeah,' said Hussein. 'How about making me black?'

'I'm black,' I said.

'No, big and black, I mean. Put me in bold. Bold and black,' he chuckled. 'Wiv capitals too.'

I thought for a moment. 'Okay,' I said. 'that's a good idea. Let's do that. But no capitals, they'd dominate too much.'

**HERE I AM. SALAM AGAIN, EVERYONE!!! I have finally got myself in my rightful place in this book. The problem's sorted, Guy. I'll write where I like. HOW I LIKE.**

But there's another issue. The book is called FOOT NOTES, Hussein.

Not my problem. You can write footnotes on my stuff if you like. Then you can know what it's like being stuck in a little box at the bottom of the page.

Hussein is an East African Muslim. I could easily picture him swathed in a white turban, hawk on his wrist, astride a sleek white mare, atop a screensaver-grade sand dune, princely in profile **I like this,** in sunlight so strong it made me scrunch up my eyes to imagine the glare. I could also see him cast as a terrorist in an American action movie **like the fake Somalians in Black Hawk Down,** or at least the younger brother of the leading bearded terrorist, who tragically gets drawn into the conspiracy. In the same movie, I may add, I am cast as the redneck mayor who claimed he wanted only justice but on the weekends was a Klansman.

At this point I knew very little about Hussein apart from where he lived and that he suffered panic attacks.

**All I knew about Guy was that he was an old white man. I was sceptical and slightly worried about the walking idea, thought** *what's he up to?*, **coz my sister, Sal, had warned me about him being a snob.**[15]

Unlike my fantasies of life on the estate, the salient features of the Hussein family household were its peaceful, loving atmosphere and the total absence of drugs, including alcohol. I picked my way between about ten pairs of children's shoes on the stairs and approached the sound of happy little boys.

Usually, I found Hussein wearing a jellabiya **I don't know what that is, but I'm a guessing Guy is talking**

---

[15] I guess you could say we both had stereotypical ideas about each other. I assumed he was a thug.

**about my khamis** in a low armchair with the children clambering over him, but today he was checking his rucksack while the three boys sat on the ornate, varnished chaise longue, their huge eyes glued to the 3.30 at Haydock Park.

The jellabiya I most associate with Hussein was faun coloured with some lacey detail at the collar, usually worn with a wooden bead necklace. It spoke of his love of Africa. Very clearly. As did the heat in the flat, which was maintained, as far as I could tell, at the same temperature as Mogadishu.

They went in for heavy net curtains, even though they were on the third floor. It looked like they didn't want to see out that much, and I couldn't really blame them. The slipped prefab slabs of the speckled concrete building opposite did not launch the spirit skyward. If you looked down you could see nappies on a flat asphalt roof. Hussein's mum didn't let the kids into the newly funded playground for fear of bad influences.

Three semi-veiled women hurried out of the kitchen towards me.

'Meester Guy, **this is all going a bit** *Django Unchained* how are you? Thank you for coming. Thank you. You know you are always welcome. Always. Sit down. Sit, sit down. Imran out of the way.' **Always have to give a seat to the elderly.**

I was led into the room with enormous furniture and a huge TV. How they had ever got those chairs and dressers up the stairs I do not know. Everywhere was crammed with possessions – in boxes, in overflowing drawers and in cupboards which wouldn't quite close.

I knew what was coming next so I sat down, mumbling something about having to be on our way, and was offered a selection of food that wouldn't disgrace the lobby of a 5-star hotel.

After I made my choice, I heard the women chattering in the kitchen, apparently, but kind of unbelievably, excited to be rustling up food for me in the middle of their day, and then Hussein's mum, a woman with a 500-watt smile, appeared with a tray. On it was a cup of tea, three different kinds of sweet pastries, lamb jalfrezi, and some saucers of other, to me, unidentifiable but irresistible comestibles. After telling me that she hoped I would like what she had made, she kindly withdrew to allow me to stuff my face unwatched. I could see how men got into being Muslims. **Convert you all, one stomach at a time.** This was not treatment I was used to. I got home and someone usually shouted *Guy – we need wine, and what's for dinner? Oh and we're out of loo paper.* I convinced myself that it would be impolite and insensitive to Muslim values if I departed before everything was eaten. It was 4pm and the meal fitted nicely between lunch and supper.

With a straining belt, it was time to leave. The little boys crowded around Hussein and he hugged each in turn.

I heard Hussein say, 'Sal, have you got the bottle ready for baby?' He kept a close eye on his sister's mothering, handing out advice and commands that would have got him clobbered in most young mum's homes I knew. Sal giggled and went about her duties.

On the way to the car Hussein waved at a guy on a bicycle who looked, to me, a bit dodgy, and called, 'Hi!'

'Do you know him?' I whispered

'He's a lot better since he got stabbed.' **Jesus, I shouldn't have said that out loud.**[16]

Hussein knew someone who had been stabbed. You would have to be in a gang to live round here. It was obvious. I tried to judge from the demeanour of the man on the bike what kind of rank Hussein held.

In my imagination I dropped into an episode of The Sweeney, and also somehow into Minder as well. Terry was safely shacked up with Rula Lenska in her blousy *pied a terre*, she who was, in the 1970s, considered hot. Mind you, so was Dennis Waterman. Which proved the whole system had gone haywire. Arthur was in the pub fencing a bulk load of chess sets with the wrong number of squares on the board, while I walked the suspect, i.e. Hussein, to my unmarked Granada. To be honest I was never going to pass as D.I. Regan. He was too hard for me. I was still in a part played by John Thaw, but Morse, in this weird TV-people-soup simmering in my brain. I was going to try and talk some sense into the lad before he took a wrong turn in life. *'Hussein,'* I would say, *'this is serious, mixing with these guys could get you in a lot of trouble. Now tell us where they meet and what they have planned, son, and I'll see what I can do for you and your mum.'*

Hussein wore tight black jeans and a slim-fit black shirt, with a black puffy coat over the top. The coat did not say country ramble, it said ten quid a hit. I couldn't tell if the jellabiya **KHAMIS Guy, please**

---

[16]Guy here, doing some time in the footnotes, learning my lesson: Later I heard about the violent white guy who knifed him. At school, the only thing he didn't take a stab at was his GCSEs.

**learn one Arab word** was in the rucksack but I hoped it wasn't. I thought it might complicate things in the Welsh borders, a notoriously conservative part of rural Britain. The rucksack itself, taken in combination with Hussein's beard was enough of an issue.

# 2.

When I first had the idea of walking with Hussein I bought him a pair of boots.

No. First, I must comment on Hussein's notes. I'm loving them. I'm thinking he's dropping his words into the text like Vibez Kartel rapping over my Kenny Rogers. **FFS, Guy. And it's spelled Vybz.**

I imagined Hussein didn't have money to hand for a pair of strong boots. I knew he was skint. He'd been out of work. I wanted him to see I was serious about our walk, and I could imagine what it would be like to be invited on a hike over tough terrain and not have the right footwear. Then I wondered if it might be offensive to offer to buy him boots. You never knew what these kinds of things freighted in different cultures. Didn't they throw footwear as a sign of disgust? I am not sure who 'they' are in that sentence. Muslims? Arabs? **Arabs** That's how bad it was in my head. Anyway, we weren't going to get any meaningful walking done in Hussein's trainers or house slippers, so I took him down to ProAdventure, an outdoor clothing and equipment shop in North Wales where we were staying for a family Christmas in 2017, to kit him out.

It was the kind of shop that sold sleeping bags, head torches and carabiners. The walls were decorated above racks of camo with fairly new posters of people wearing the merchandise. In one photo there was a couple of blokes with helmets on, standing on a limestone ridge with a bit of British wilderness beyond, and in another a clean-cut, nuclear family crouching by a tent. These people were all white. Standing by Hussein that fact kind of hung in the air, like a faint smell.

I had noticed that the number of black men and women featured in all advertising was increasing as the industry made amends for the racial outrages of the past. When I saw a black barmaid in a Guinness ad pulling pints in a Dublin pub it smacked of black-washing, and prompted me to Google what percentage of the Irish population was black. Was that being thorough or racist? I've certainly never been accused of the first. It was 1% by the way. Then I remembered Phil Lynott, the black and Irish rock-star, and anyway, why not over-represent black people in Ireland in ads? What possible harm could it do? And think of all the good it could do. My initial resistance to it was troubling.

I couldn't help noticing how Hussein stood out in ProAdventure **I stand out pretty much anywhere outside London** Let me come to the point: it was a white person's shop. There was nothing in that shop I would expect to see a young black man wearing. Or indeed an old one. I recently tried to research how many of the British people who hiked and climbed in the countryside were black. The Ramblers Association did not collect that information, shamefully, when they had time to count the average number of miles walked on foot a year by British folk (197) and many other silly bits of information. They failed to ask the question of how many BAME people venture onto out country's footpaths. I suggest that they are hiding the truth because it is ugly. Only 2% of black people live in rural areas. The British countryside is virtually a no-go area for black people.

Not surprisingly, Hussein looked ill at ease and a bit lost amongst the waterproof trousers and gaiters. I hope he writes a footnote about the moment we shared in that shop. I didn't know if he felt excluded. I would. **Anyone would, Guy. I felt like I was on another planet. Plus, I didn't really know you then, or what we were doing there.** I asked the assistant, a young woman with bright red cheeks, to show me the range of walking boots. Hussein was evincing the difficulties of being bought footwear by a virtual stranger. I respected that, and wanted to be tactful, hard as you may find that to believe. While I was shown the boots, Hussein hovered over a display cabinet of hunting and camping knives. The assistant glanced at him, and then back at the boots. I presumed she was imagining Hussein not skinning rabbits but mugging pedestrians. That was in my head. Nearly all of this stuff was in my head. **The knife collection is all I remember from the shop, mostly due to *Crocodile Dundee*. I have always wanted one of those, but obviously can't own one as I live in London, and the only knife you need here are kitchen knives. They do for everything.**

The stuff in my head. Where did it come from? Was it wrong? Should I be lying about it? Was I alone?

To Hussein I said, 'Pick any pair from those two shelves.'

He selected a pair in the middle **I didn't have a clue what constitutes good walking boots so I was stuck** between choosing a more expensive pair or going down the middle of the price range without any attention-seeking design features. I had previously worried he would look like a crack-dealing pimp, and now I was concerned they were too dull. I was in a state of muted hysteria.

'I think you should try them on,' I said.

He sat down, still in his puffy anorak, and started taking off a trainer. Removing your shoes in a public place is a vulnerable act. I gave him some space. I felt protective; I wanted to show him how easy it was to walk the British countryside, where black folk usually don't ramble. And I was going to do something about that fact. Starting by buying Hussein a good pair of walking boots. Then writing about our adventure.

Was the shop actively trying to exclude black girls, boys, men and women from outdoor activities? That was ridiculous. Or did black British people not want to kayak or rock climb or camp? **Yes.** That was even more ridiculous. **It's true.** Or was it just that black citizens had had to fight their way, building by building, through the heavily defended towns and suburbs of racism, and were only now regrouping before tackling the countryside? So why did Hussein look so out of place in there? I can only conclude that it was entirely in my mind.

I bought the boots, Hussein seemed happy, and we drove back up to where we staying in the hills.

Three weeks later, back in Tottenham, Hussein was wearing his new walking boots as we made our way to my car. We loaded his rucksack, puffy coat and he got in, clutching a plastic jug.

'What's that for?' I asked.

'In case I vomit.'

'You won't need that,' I said as we eased out of the parking space. 'I drive very gently.'

He glanced at me and retched into the jug. In stop-go traffic on the North Circular Road, Hussein said, 'It's got worse, Guy, cos I got a phobia about being sick, as well as one about travelling in a car.'

'What?' I said.

'I have a fear of being sick. That's what I am telling you, Guy. The fear makes me vomit.' It's called emetophobia.

He stopped being sick by the time we neared the turn off for the A40. Naturally, I was silently diagnosing and analysing him all the time. He opened the window, dry heaved, and spotted a big white building. 'Ah, Chinese supermarket, that's maybe where Mum gets the Chinese rice. It's the best rice.'

'Do you like London?' I asked him.

'Mum says I like it too much,' he replied.

A clue – I thought.

Considering the social and racial chasm that apparently separated us, the three hour trip to my house in Somerset was surprisingly easy, and Hussein leant back and took in the wide open plains of Wiltshire and the wooded hills and deep lanes of Somerset without a single vomit.

We overnighted in my house and drove the next day up to Shropshire. Hussein asked if he could play music from his phone.

'I'm starting with old music and going to get more recent,' he said above the Marvin Gaye. I admit I am a bit of a racist when it comes to music: it has to be black. I wasn't disappointed by Hussein's selection. As we crossed the Severn Estuary into Wales, he played music from Nigeria, Kenya and then London, all of it good, all of it black.

# 3.

The Offa's Dyke Path is an ancient right of way that runs the length of the English/Welsh border, from Chepstow to the Wirral, a distance of 177 miles in total. We were going to knock off a section in the middle, on a hike that I calculated would take about four or five days, sleeping in local hotels and B&Bs where we found them.

Our starting point was a grand country house called Linley, near Bishop's Castle, where my friend Ewen and his wife Beth held court. We approached down an arrow-straight avenue of double planted beech trees, whose considerable promise was fully met by the house at its head. A huge Georgian palace reared up in front of us, beside a lake.

'Does Ewen own all this?' Hussein asked.

'And thousands of acres,' I said, 'so both of you live on massive estates,' I couldn't resist adding.

The house was undergoing extensive restoration and we walked across floors covered in plastic and through temporary doors in plywood panels. As Ewen showed me and Hussein around, I wondered what Hussein was thinking. I was now always wondering what Hussein was thinking. I guessed he had only seen a house like this on TV or in a movie. **I had actually been to this house before, with Guy's son. But yeah, it's a big crib.**

We ate a game stew of pheasant and partridge, and drank claret at supper. Hussein didn't drink. But I didn't get that disapproving vibe that I sometimes get from my friends who have given up the booze. He didn't meet my eye every time I took a deep glug, for instance.

After dinner, Beth, a woman of action in mustard corduroy trousers, unfolded some OS maps on a big table and we scoped out a route. It was easy to see Linley on the map, because its avenue was the straightest line on the thing. The Offa's Dyke Path was about 6 miles to the west, a snake of dashes heading up the paper. We could cut across fields and through woods to meet it, or walk a little south to Bishop's Castle and then along a lane on a ridge to strike the path south of Montgomery.

We decided to take the southern route along the longer but tarmacked road, because we were idiots who knew little about long-distance hiking. It was before I learnt, the hard way, that the best option on foot is always the shortest.

The night before we set off, I drowned in an old country house mattress on a four-poster bed, resurfacing before dawn to dress and to pack my small knapsack. I put on two pairs of socks, a thin pair and a skiing pair. Downstairs, Hussein had been up for some time and was standing in the corner of the kitchen looking hunted.

'Anxiety level?' I asked. I had already established a short-hand scale between one and ten so he could share his difficulties with me.

'Six.'

We'd only ever got to a seven before, when I thought we were going to run out of petrol on the M4 near Cardiff. I looked him in the eye.

'Don't you worry, we'll soon have you hearty and happy again, down in the twos and threes, and on your way back to finish that degree of yours. The aim of this adventure, my friend, is to get your mojo back, and failure is not an option.'

'Do you have a water bottle?' he asked me.

'No,' I said, 'quite deliberately. And we carry no food either.'

'It's a forty-mile hike, Guy.'

'I know, but I want us to have contact with the locals as we pass through. This way we will have to interact with people. It's much better.'

'No water?' Hussein said.

'But don't worry, my friend, because I have this,' I held up an empty enamel mug. **100% thought you'd gone mad**. He looked at it and then at me. 'We don't want to have to carry lots of stuff,' I said. 'We'll trust in the road; it will look after us. I can always find a spring. Have faith.'

Over the next few days, I saw many emotions on Hussein's friendly face, but most of them at the anxious, apprehensive and even appalled end of the feelings chart. Right then, he just looked confused and mildly alarmed. I patted him on the back and said, 'Don't worry, it'll be fine. You'll see. England is a place of abundance and generosity.'

We set off into the warm and drizzly September morning. The verge and hedges were heavy with summer growth, and the cobwebs festooned with droplets of moisture. Our host decided to walk the first leg with us, as he said he knew a short cut across the fields to Bishop's Castle. We walked down a lane three abreast with a bounce in our step. The open road and adventure lay ahead. Spirits were high.

A tedious impulse made me look for my phone, which after going through my pockets I realised I had left on a mahogany chest of drawers in my bedroom. It was a sign of how relaxed I was that I decided not to ask for someone to drive out with it immediately. I was free.

After leaving a hamlet by an overgrown stile under some gloomy oaks, Ewen lead us onto a footpath which petered out on a sloping field. One moment the path was clearly there, the next it was three possibilities, none of which looked reliable. Rather than retracing our steps we took our chance with the right-hand path, lost it in the corner of the field and had to break into a ruined coniferous wood littered with pheasant pens and feeders. I crouched low and waddled between the trees, trying to avoid being stabbed by broken branches and grasped by brambles, sliding down a steep incline into a bog. With the crack of breaking wood and the suck and gulp of boots in mud we struggled across the swamp, crawled up a steep ridge, forced our way through a rusted fence and found ourselves in a ploughed field. Hussein was having trouble with his puffy jacket on the barbed wire. With kilos of mud glued to our boots we trudged up a long climb, down another one and ended up in a huge and noxious puddle of liquid cow shit with a line of bullocks nudging their way towards us.

Ewen looked at the farm buildings to the right of the animals and said, 'Oh – here we are, I know where we are.'

I think Hussein was alarmed by the cows, **my only other experience with cows before this was being chased by a skinny white cow in Kenya, and now I was in a field with thirty to forty well-fed cows. Who wouldn't be 'alarmed'?** but didn't say anything. I was anxious, so led Hussein gently along a breeze block wall to a gate we escaped over, alighting in a farm yard between some machinery and pallets of chemicals. I could see tarmac beyond the farm house, so headed confidently towards it. It was about 50 metres of hard standing to get to the public road.

I turned to see Hussein hesitating. His jacket was muddy **or covered in cow poo** and nicked in one or two places. I was suddenly aware that waltzing through a stranger's private property was a different proposition for Hussein than for me and Ewen. We looked like we were out taking the morning air and had got a little lost, Hussein looked like he was on the run from a G4S van. When he stepped onto the concrete it suddenly looked like a 500 metre walk, not 50. He, nevertheless, followed us across the yard, past an office in a barn with an open door which I prayed a man was not going to appear in. I felt myself walking faster towards the gate, propelled by a fear of other people's racism. Was that also a sign of mine? Then I thought it looked like we were running away, so slowed down. By the time we got back onto tarmac, I was worn out and covered in scratches.

The road into Bishop's Castle ran past a fancy new housing estate. The sun had come out, the temperature had risen and Hussein was sweating. The puffy coat, with padding sprouting from its holes, was now slung over his arm. We looked like we'd been on the road for weeks. I decided that the coat was going to make things worse so I advised Hussein to give it to Ewen when Beth came to pick him up and take him back home. Hussein handed it over reluctantly.

**I remember this because Ewen offered me his Ralphy jacket for the walk but he had mentioned it had previously belonged to his deceased dad, and so had sentimental value, so I had to turn it down because if the first couple of hours was a teaser of what was to come, that jacket would not have looked good when I handed it back.**

I reasoned to myself that the weather looked like it was getting warmer and dryer, and the puffy coat was going to be far too heavy. We would buy another lightweight anorak in one of the many outdoor shops that I, in my imagination, presumed studded the route of the Offa's Dyke Path. Also, the knee length coat was not saying what we wanted. Without it, you noticed Hussein's new walking boots more and they clearly said, *I am a rambler.* The coat said, *I'm scoping the lock on your barns. I'm after your strimmer.*

We bid goodbye to Ewen and Beth, and were suddenly on our own in the middle of the road, with the long walk ahead. As the car drew away the sky clouded over. Hussein looked at me in my fully waterproof anorak.

We took a selfie with my phone, which I had weakly asked Diana to bring me from the house, and walked west out of Bishop's Castle up a long, straight hill. At the three mile point it turned out to be a grinding climb which you wouldn't notice in a car, but on foot took its toll. We didn't talk. I just wanted to get to the footpath and start walking north in the direction of our destination.

A few cars passed us. I started noticing the faces of the drivers and passengers. Most were neutral until they got close enough to see that Hussein was black. We were in deep Shropshire, hiking on a country lane, wearing just a fleece in Hussein's case. This was not what they were used to seeing on their highways and byways. Some looked confused and seemed to strain their eyes to assess more who we might be, and what we might be up to. One woman passenger I was sure I could see craning her neck to look up the road behind us for a broken down car. I wished I had a petrol can in my hand to reassure them. Even when they smiled, which many did, I had never seen a smile quite like that. I think the term in linguistics is over-compensation. I don't know what it is in the science of facial expression. Over-beaming? I have used it myself. It's the expression that says, *Welcome! It's fine to walk on this lane, really. I am sure you're a nice young man, and, well, it's so good to see you with him. If a man like you in a decent waxed Barbour and boots with laces is overseeing him, then that's okay by us. In fact, it's more than okay. It's a wonderful thing to see diversity amongst the hedgerows. We don't see enough of it.* (Although her husband, a small man with a grey 'tache in beige said with his smile: *that's quite far enough.*) His wife's eyes sparkled. I read from them: *Please remember my friendly smile when you pass our immaculate and unattended bungalow a mile down the road as we won't be back from Sainsbury's for about two hours.* No driver simply lifted a finger off the steering wheel the way they did in Somerset, when I was on my own, to denote casual, tribal acceptance.

The lifted finger was a micro-acceptance, and these were micro-warnings. I asked Hussein if he noticed them and he said I was making them up in my head.

'Don't you face racist behaviour all the time?' I asked. 'Big stuff, I mean, like name calling?'

'Yeah, there might have been cases, like, but none I can remember,' he said. 'Nothing heavy.'

I stared at him. This was the first inkling I had that Hussein wasn't going to fit neatly into the picture of the two of us I had planned for the walk and, I must admit, this book.

'Really?' I said, wanting more, but he had turned and was walking away up the lane.

I thought, *a twenty-one-year-old black Muslim from Tottenham who didn't have a long catalogue of racist complaints?* It must be a million to one against finding that person. Or he didn't want to tell me, or he was in denial about it. Maybe I should swap him for one of his friends. The one on the bike, for instance. Find a more normal black guy to work my magic on.

I looked at Hussein's spindly legs under his fleece. His head was bowed forwards with the exertion of the hill. He looked committed to the walk. I smiled. We were in this together. He was untypical. Well, he wasn't stereotypical. That might create a problem for some, but for me, I decided, it would enrich the story. I strongly suspected I would find out in due course why Hussein didn't want to talk about racist incidents. There was plenty of time. We had forty miles ahead of us. And, as we were soon to do literally, we had metaphorically gone off my map; it felt exciting and unpredictable, the way life should be if it's being lived properly.

At the top of the hill, I silently blessed Hussein when he asked for a rest. We leant against a gate and looked out over the wealthy farms of the valley floor with their barns, fields and copses. In the misty distance the Long Mynd looked like a giant asleep in the landscape.

'Isn't this grand?' I said.

'As you know I've got a phobia about silence,' Hussein said.

'What?'

'I hate silence. It does my head in. I told you.'

'You didn't,' I said.

'Yes I did, Guy. You must have been not listening.'

This could be a long few days, I thought to myself as I unfolded the OS map from my pocket. I didn't have a transparent pouch hanging from my neck. It was part of my *we are not ramblers, we are travellers in this land* vibe. We are going from point A to point B. Not from point A to point A, like hobby walkers. We weren't doing a two-hour circuit back to the car park, walking the dog or trying to lose some weight. I didn't disapprove of the rambling middle classes of Britain, with their Gore-Tex, gaiters and ski sticks, but I didn't want to be one of them. I was not in their movie. I was in mine, which was set a long time before lightweight walking boots and map pouches, sometime around the fourteenth century, and Hussein was played by Morgan Freeman in a turban and I carried a long-bow and a quiver of arrows. We were returning to my castle after being believed long dead by our families, there to settle some scores and rescue my wife and children. Combat and hardship in the holy land (where we met and bonded in the prequel) have grizzled us.

After a struggle with the map and refolding it a couple of times, I realised we had not only failed to traverse the first crease, we had barely moved from the square we started in. I turned it over to see how far we had to go before we got to the Offa's Dyke Path where the walk proper would begin, and then how far it was to Llangollen, our final destination. I traced with my finger where we were, how far we had travelled and then – with a lot of unfolding and then getting out another whole map, and then another until there were three on the gate – we found the town of Llangollen.

'That can't be right,' I said.

'It's a very long way, Guy,' Hussein said.

'Nonsense. We'll be there the day after tomorrow.'

'I don't think so,' said Hussein. 'I think it's too far.'

'No defeatist talk,' said I.

Around about then, it started getting gusty which made folding the maps back up even more difficult. They had all put on weight when I stuffed them in my pocket.

'I don't think you've done that right.' Hussein said, helpfully.

'It'll have to do.'

'It might tear and then we could get lost,' he said.

I pulled the map out again and opened it up. The wind whipped at the paper which billowed out from my arms and then snapped into my face. While I struggled with this cartoon squeezebox, the rain attacked in short, aggressive bursts. Hussein huddled in his fleece. I suggested we take cover under a tree. There we stood as I watched rain drops come through the canopy and bloom on his absorbent garment. He looked chilly and exhausted. Already. Of the 40 mile trip, we had covered about 800 metres in the direction we needed to go.

The trees and verge sparkled when the sun came out. We walked on. Another squadron of rain clouds cruised towards us over the hilly landscape.

'Looks like they're coming our way,' Hussein said.

'Do you want my anorak?' I asked, rhetorically.

He didn't want it, so I felt pleased and guilty.

We finally got onto the same fold on the map as the Offa's Dyke footpath, and took a lane diagonally towards it. The sky had cleared and the plain and hills of the border country were well lit in front of us. Hussein said he was thirsty. I was a bit thirsty too, so I turned my back to Hussein and asked him to take the enamel cup out of my backpack.

'Now we just look on the map for a river,' I said, extracting the bulge from my pocket, 'and head towards it.'

We both tried to find where we were on it again. We stared at it, then I opened it up and refolded it a couple of times.

'We are still on the first page, Guy,' Hussein said. 'That's disappointing.'

'Yes,' I said, folding back the concertina I had so hopefully opened.

I remembered that Ewen and Beth had suggested a few places to have lunch in Montgomery. But I saw it was hours away.

Hussein studied the map. 'I can't see a river, Guy.'

'That'll be because we're on a hill. Down on the plain we'll find a nice clean brook, don't you worry. Pellucid, it will be. Crystalline. You have a treat in store. So good not to be drinking from plastic or having water laced with chlorine or fluoride.'

'Chlorine makes water safe to drink.'

'Bah,' I said, 'nothing purer than the water from these hills,' I said. 'We just have to locate a source.'

We folded up the map and walked on in silence. Further on down the hill I saw what looked like a stream running down a field and crossing under the road.

I searched under the hedge for it amongst some faded litter and oily mud.

'This looks promising,' I said.

'I don't want a drink from a ditch,' Hussein said.

I stared at the trickle.

'Yes,' I said. 'We'll find something better than that.' We trudged on. The sun was out, the land drying after rain. I sensed in Hussein's silence a scepticism about my expedition leadership skills. He wasn't sullen, exactly, but I felt that what little enthusiasm he had ever had for our walk was rapidly dwindling. I didn't have much time to find water.

**When Guy mentioned this walk, I thought zero chance this thing would happen. We would probably do a walk around his house and that's about it. As you have gathered, he is a big talker, right? When we first got to Linley, I thought *shit we're doing this*. That's when I first started truly thinking we might not only finish it but would go on to do other walks – he talked about doing one in London and one in Africa, which was slightly exciting. But, early on in this first walk, I started waking up to how bad Guy was at planning things.**

I played for time. 'I grew up in the country,' I said. 'My grandfather owned farms. That's how I know about things like water.'

'My family owned land too,' Hussein said.

'Really?' I said. 'Like, more than just a garden?'

'Yes. More than just a garden,' Hussein said politely. 'Part of my family are East African nobility.'

'What?' I said.

'That's a surprise to you, I imagine. What were you expecting?'

He laid down the gauntlet. I decided not to lie. 'Well, I thought, er, you know, you were a bit more ordinary and ...'

'... poor?'

I nodded.

'Because we are from Africa?'

'Well, er,' I said, 'I assumed you were probably economic migrants to the UK.'

He paused a moment and then said, matter of factly, 'Some of the women in my family are royal princesses. We had lands. Great Granny gave half our lands to a mosque. Great Granny was a good slave owner.'

'What did you say?'

'Granny gave half our lands to the mosque.'

'Did you say you were good slave owners? Is there such a thing?'

'The myth in the family is that we were good slave owners.'[1]

---

[1]At this point in the first draft of the manuscript, my writer friend, Claude, pointed out to me that the book proposal I had shown the publisher, which promised a meeting of racial, social and political opposites, was somewhat compromised by Hussein saying he came from a Royal, slave-owning family. My first reaction was to think it was a bit racist to harbour preconditions about Hussein. He is not from a long line of abused and down-trodden black people. How unsettling!

'Oh,' said I.

'The British were not, I think.'

'It's just that I assumed all slavery must be bad.'

'No, not all,' he said. **I don't remember saying that. I do come from a family that owned slaves, and my understanding is that the family takes a similar stance to American slave owners, where they all claim to have been good slave owners treating slaves well. We (Mum's dad) apparently gave them land and freed them and the kids and grandkids still live on those lands. I don't think slavery was ever good.**

'So you're, like, an aristocrat?' I said.

He held himself with great dignity and said, 'We were a big, rich and old land-owning family.' He swallowed, 'but we lost or gave away all its wealth and most of its land, so we have only pride left.'

I nodded. 'I'm sorry,' I said.

He turned and walked on ahead of me. I decided to give him some space until I realised I might not catch up with him. It took half an hour before I came alongside again. He, like I, had been thinking about what he had told me, because he said, 'An inheritance of only pride isn't good for the first generation that has to actually go out and find work with zero qualifications.'

'You mean like you?'

'Yes.'

For the first time I felt radically different from Hussein. When I was twenty-three I was raring to go, crashing around life making lots of mistakes, but with loads of optimism and plans. He was so resigned to a fate he had decreed for himself in which he was powerless. Was that being Hussein, or being African, or being African in Britain?

36

'But that's why you must finish your uni course,' I said. 'And if you do, it'll make you feel great and help you get on in life.'

'I never even wanted to go to university, I wanted to drop out of sixth form after the first year,' he said.

'Why? Why give up?'

'Because I had enough of the education system, with its never-ending stages. First you do your GCSEs then you take your A-levels, then off to do your degree, followed by a Masters, then apparently a PhD. And at the beginning of each stage the institution tells you this is all you need in life then you can get a job, but at the end, after your pass, you get told in this climate you need to get to the next level to stand out because everyone else has the exact same qualifications. Sure, a degree would be useful if I wanted to do a STEM subject, but after GCSEs I'd lost interest in maths, I was now more interested in history than any other subject.'

I translated this to myself as: *I was never properly taught at school. I never got the help from parents who had passed A-levels and got on to university. They were too busy surviving as newly arrived immigrants. I didn't have teachers who had time to talk to me about my options, or a friendship group who were travelling in the direction of university and a good job, in whose wake I would be pulled.*

Nothing else sense made sense to me. Hussein was clearly bright. But what an opportunity for me this was! The story was on a new and unexpected trajectory. The prince in exile. This was indeed a book of redemption. I didn't mention any of that then; it was time to lighten the mood.

'So your family are all toffs?' I laughed.

'Not kings and queens, just lords and ladies, in a society where titles are passed down from mother to child. But we had two generations of giving land away. The kids and grandkids stepped in and reduced how much, but by then it was mostly over. And other things happened, so we had to leave our lands.'

'Other things happened' I took to be a reference to the turbulent, chaotic and violent political events of the last forty years in Somalia, Eritrea and Ethiopia which had stripped the family of what was left of their possessions and turned them into refugees, fleeing for safety in Kenya and then London. Hussein's family were already in exile in Kenya when he was born, and he had never set foot in the Horn of Africa. Its dry plains and red hills were not in his memory, but would always be in his blood.

'Maybe after this walk through the borders, we could do a walk in Somalia, and you can show me where your lands were.'

'We can't go to Somalia; there's too much crime.'

'I came to Tottenham. It can't be worse than that.' I said.

He was not amused.

'It's under Sharia law,' he said.

'That could be bad for me,' I said.

I inferred from his silence he wasn't altogether disapproving of that.

I thought about his high-born background. How did I end up picking an inner-city youth with this back story? It was categorically not what I had promised to the publisher. In that way, it was not helpful. But of course, hundreds, thousands probably, of black people in Europe had a story like Hussein's. There were black aristocrats all around me whenever I went to a city. Some (like most of the white aristocrats) a bit down on their luck and fortune, but nevertheless sons and daughters of princes and princesses, lords and ladies, like Hussein. What was unusual about Hussein was that he actually knew his family story, and could tell it to me, because the information had not been destroyed by slavery, that hydraulic crusher of history. Hussein's family were Ethiopians, and had not been stolen and sold to the plantations in the Americas. They had been on the other side of Africa, 4000 sandy and inhospitable miles from the crimes on the Ivory coast. Another assumption about him was punctured.

After a mile or two of walking, during which I let these facts settle, I began to feel pleased that the black youth from the council flat in Tottenham I had picked to walk with and write about turned out to be a goddam royal.

I looked at the map and let out a laugh. 'Look, the George and Dragon,' I tapped the paper. 'A pub! At the next crossroads. We need to celebrate your news. And it's about time for a drink.'

'I don't drink alcohol,' Hussein said

'Don't worry about that,' I said. 'I do.' I looked at my watch, expecting it to be lunch time. It said 10.20. 'Come on,' I said, undeterred.

When we reached the George and Dragon, we found it had been converted into a bijou retirement cottage. One cartwheel was stuck on the wall. And there was no one in. Hussein leant against a gate on the other side of the lane.

'Guy, you didn't plan this very well,' he said.

'There's sure to be somewhere in the next hamlet,' I said, thinking simultaneously *what hamlet nowadays has a shop or a pub?*

We trudged along for another hour, passing a middle-aged couple walking a terrier on a long lead. We got another couple of surprised smiles.

'Why didn't you ask them?' Hussein asked.

I had been too shy. My tin cup felt stupid. 'They weren't the right type,' I said. 'It needs to be someone at home, anyway, with a tap.'

Finally, thank God, or Allah, whichever one came up with it, we approached a neat bungalow with a well-tended garden and a car on a tarmac drive. A wheelbarrow half full of weeds stood on a path. I walked the concrete paving to the front door. Hussein hung back. I don't know why. Had I indicated with my hand for him to stay where he was because I thought it might improve our chances? It was possible. I had worked out by then that I was actively trying to prevent any racist behaviour from strangers. But was that, in itself, enabling racism? I rang the bell on the glass porch and waited to see a blur on the door. None appeared and I assumed no one was in. Unless they were lurking. Maybe an old lady was standing in the hall, too scared to open the door to a stranger, particularly with a black youth hanging around the other side of the hedge.

'No luck,' I said.

As I walked back to Hussein, I saw a garden tap on a trellis with a hose attached to it which disappeared round the back of the house. I might have gone to look for the end of the pipe but, in these circumstances, didn't want to wander round the back of any buildings in case it looked like I was searching for a way in. Also, the hose looked old and I thought any water that issued from it would taste of plastic, unless I ran the water for a long time, and that conjured up the image of me in the back yard shouting instructions to Hussein at the tap, as the police, summoned by the old lady, rolled up. There was too much to go wrong. Being thought a house breaker was something I had never worried about before. Hussein saw the tap, too. I looked to see how easy it would be to unscrew the pipe off the tap. There was a lot of thread and twisting such a long hose would be cumbersome. I pictured trying to reattach it quickly as a car came into the drive.

'I don't feel good about this,' I said. 'I'd rather not take any water without asking.'

'It's water, Guy. Water's a human right.'

I thought, *what is it with these locals that they don't have any corner shops? Where do they get fruits, bottled water and snacks?*

We got back on the tarmac which, after a fall of rain, glistened black. The lane sloped down for a mile to a wooden way marker on a stile in the hedge. A yellow oak leaf pointed in both directions to Offa's Dyke footpath. Tired, thirsty and demoralised, we had reached the start of our walk.

# 4.

Offa was a Saxon king who decided to build a wall to keep the Welsh out of England. It was a phenomenal engineering achievement: 100 miles long, 20 metres wide and 2.4 metres high. Built before the invention of the wheelbarrow. In the era of wooden spades. With an English workforce. Either there was something very scary about the Welsh, or it was an extraordinary act of paranoia. The drovers' track that ran beside the dyke is almost the only remains of the dyke you can see today. The track is designated as a footpath now, but as Hussein and I walked north I could see that it had once been wide enough for a horse drawn vehicle. In places I saw rough cobbles under the earth, and often noticed that the oldest trees on the path were set wide enough to let a cart pass between them. We were on an ancient way, walked by humans, often traders, for centuries. Nowadays, the path was used by people walking for leisure. Since Hussein's elevation to royalty, and my trouble with the hose pipe, I had recast the movie that was playing in my mind. As we trod north under the canopy of leaves we were now a royal Arab Prince, played by Omar Sharif, and Baldrick. **The only reference I got so far. Omar Sharif. We share a surname.**

Just after we crossed the border into Wales, and I had delivered a short but moving (I thought) lecture on the glories of the Union, Hussein spotted a sign that said B&B Vacancies.

'There's a house, shall we ask there for water?' He said.

After the debacle with the garden hose, I was hoping for a pub or a shop, but I had to admit that the map made it look like it was unbroken countryside until the next town, about 18 inches away, and it took us about an hour to do 4 inches.

'Good idea,' I said, and steeled myself for another ordeal. Upland sheep farms were usually dilapidated, bankrupt outrages against animal welfare and the olfactory sense, manned by broken men worn down by years of unprofitable, backbreaking work. But this place was a well-tended upland sheep farm, with a neat old farmhouse, dangling with hanging baskets, and a metal table and chair outside which looked like they were recently bought and never used. I guessed the B&B venture was a new attempt to make some cash. I saw an ATV, a Land Rover, and thinking that someone from the house might be watching me, immediately looked away so they didn't think I was eying them up. I went round to the side, through a gate, beckoning Hussein to come with me, then rang the bell and stood well back from the door. A dark blur and then a small middle-aged lady in a pinafore came to the door. She looked at me and Hussein, and smiled.

I held out the cup. Suddenly aware of Hussein behind me. I felt like I was in an Oxfam ad.

'Hello, we are on a walk and stupidly didn't pack enough water,' **made a conscious choice not to pack any**

**water** I said, not glancing at Hussein, 'and are thirsty and I wondered if we could have some water? Do you have a tap in the yard we could use?'

'Why, of course. Pass me that, I'll go and fill it in the kitchen.'

I was astonished because, as far as I could tell, she either hadn't noticed Hussein, which was unlikely, or, she didn't think Hussein required any special treatment or reaction.

She returned with the enamel mug brimming with water.

'Thank you very much,' Hussein and I said together.

I drank half, and didn't know whether to hand the rest to Hussein or to ask her to make a second journey.

'Drink it up and I'll get your friend another. Would you like one?'

'Yes please,' said Hussein.

She came back and passed the mug to Hussein with a kind smile. A small, slightly bent man in a checked shirt with well combed hair appeared at the door. I realised we had disturbed their Sunday lunch. He glanced at me and then at Hussein. He didn't look any more suspicious of Hussein than he did of me; I figured that as a Welsh hill farmer he didn't have time to categorise outsiders. If we weren't Welsh and from the hill, we were all foreigners.

'I'm so sorry to disturb your lunch.'

'That's all right. Have you lost your water bottle?'

'We didn't bring one. Idiotic! I don't know how that happened.'

He gave me a sharp look. Hussein nodded.

'I'll give you one. I've got a spare.' He went off towards the barn. Hussein looked at me. The lady came back with a third full cup which I drank. She refilled it from a jug for Hussein. 'You on the path?' she asked.

'Yes,' I said, 'going north all the way to Llangollen. Phew.'

'Where did you start?'

'Near Bishop's Castle,' then I played a master stroke. 'Linley Hall.'

'Linley Hall?' she said, 'oh yes.'

'My friend lives there,' I said. I thought it would relax her, but it did the opposite. I realised it was five miles away, and in England, which meant Ewen, too, was an outsider.

'Here's a bottle,' her husband said. 'I'll go and fill it.' He went into the house.

We left with the full bottle in an elastic loop on Hussein's rucksack.

Back on the path, we walked in silence, eventually stopping for a rest beside the corduroy bark of an oak of full girth. I swept my arm at the leaf-framed vista. Pools of sunshine, driven on a warm wind, moved over the patchwork of fields and woods.

'Now, you have to admit, that that's a hell of a view. Beautiful, eh?' I said.

'It's okay,' said Hussein.

'It says one word to me,' I said, 'England! Our country, my dear friend Hussein. England.'

'Isn't that Wales, Guy?'

'Britain, I should say.'

'Yeah,' said Hussein.

'As I say, we're all included,' I said.

# 5.

The stiles, gates, fences, hinges and latches of the Offa's Dyke Path were firm and strong. The skill of British farmers at obscuring footpaths is generally more developed than their talent with livestock, but none dared to dispute this right of way – proof that tourism was superseding farming as a political force.

Every time we started wondering if we were lost and thought we had to get the maddening map out again, either Hussein or I would spot a little yellow oak with a reassuring arrow etched onto a post, and as we looked in the direction it pointed I usually saw, beside the rotting fences and slack, black barbed wire of the farmer's own work, a neat new stile and, beyond, the metal kissing gate installed by the Offa's Dyke footpath people. I felt a gratitude to the men and women who had come out in their ATV and trailer and hammered in the posts and gates to keep us on track.

We actually make some progress and by 1 p.m. (I remember at this point checking the map to see where and how far Montgomery was. It was 2 or 3 pages away meaning we weren't even half way to the point where we thought we'd be having lunch) had advanced over the fold in the map that had grown grimy from being looked at so often and were heading for map 2. We came up alongside a crowd of static caravans in a high walled garden of a castle, whose faux Victorian battlements we glimpsed through the Scots pines.

There were scores of caravans, neatly presented, with well cut grass, tarmac drives and small timber decks and awnings. I guessed these had put their roots down in the 70s when it was easy to get permission to sprinkle them around the place, particularly for men who lived in a big house with land to spare. As we got closer to the red stone buildings, we saw a sign for tea room, restaurant and hotel. We left the path and slogged towards a rest. On the ballustraded steps leading up to the baronial front door a large party of men, in proper outdoor wear, stood watching Hussein and me staggering towards them.

We were quite muddy and wet so I suggested we removed our waterproof trousers and boots in the porch. The sound of a full and welcoming bar could be heard whenever guests came in or out of the door.

I said, 'You should leave the rucksack, too,' to Hussein.

'No. It has everything in it,' he said.

'I'm leaving my jacket,' I said.

'You might get it stolen,' said Hussein.

'Not here,' I said, but when I thought of all the caravans I decided he might be right. He picked up his rucksack.

'Don't put it on,' I said.

'Why?' he asked.

'Well,' I lowered my voice. 'It's just that you might, you might, look a bit like a terrorist,' I said. This was partly the reason I had made the stupid decision not to carry any food or water. I nursed a romantic desire to trust the road but I also did not want Hussein's rucksack to look too bulky and scary. **I don't look Arab, the last terrorist that looked like me in the west I think failed and burnt his balls off. I'll write you a footnote about it.**[1]

He smiled at me, sort of pityingly, I thought, and walked ahead carrying his knapsack at his side into the welcoming warmth of a Sunday lunch being served to many guests. He proceeded into the bar with one empty table in the corner. I stuck close, looking as Christian as possible by smiling at the beer fonts. There were about twenty people in there. All white. That was the kind of thing I had started noticing.

Hussein sat down on the curved purple banquette. I went to the bar and got myself a beer and Hussein a Coca Cola.

As I put them on the table, I noticed how anxious Hussein looked.

'Stress level?' I asked.

'Six.' He reported.

---

[1] For us Somalis living in Tottenham, the trouble is not being pressured to join ISIS or Al Qaeda, but to join MI5. A group of Somali community leaders had to make representations to the Secret Service to stop them targeting us. Some Somali men were approached twice in one day, just going about their everyday business. As for extremists? Their recruitment department wasn't so well funded, and I never got approached. I did once go to a mosque in Mombasa that had been raided by the Kenyan security services. I would not be a terrorist, but I do get the whole 'one man's terrorist is another man's freedom fighter' and that some terrorists have crossed over and become celebrated figures, Mandela being one. I'm sure Gandhi would have been a terrorist to the Brits like the Mau Mau in Kenya. And the Americans are currently negotiating with the Taliban.

'Six?' I said, 'I'm sorry, about that. Is it because of being thought a terrorist?'

He said, 'It's worse than people thinking I am a terrorist.'

I glanced up at the pub; lots of white faces looked away from me.

'What could be worse than that?'

Hussein took a sip of Coke and looked at me. 'People thinking I'm your boyfriend?' he said.

'Shit,' I said, and took a long drink of beer.

There were two empty chairs at our table and plenty of room for another party, but I noticed quite a few people waiting by the door, apparently looking for a seat, some of whom looked like groups of two.

Opposite Hussein and me, under a print of the castle, three couples were crowded round a table for two. I could see what was going on. I looked at Hussein and he gave me an encouraging smile which, though a little bleak, said *Don't worry, Guy, we'll get through this*, and for which I loved him. I delved into my knapsack to extract some stuff that would prove it wasn't a bomb, though the first thing that came out were the wires for my charger and my cylindrical back up battery which seemed to me exactly what I imagined components of an IED to look like.

I glanced at the people squeezed together on the banquette so as to avoid, I assumed, sitting next to me and Hussein.

The crowd at the door was disturbed when two ladies, one with steel walking sticks and a dramatic swerve to her gait, and the other wildly obese, shoved their way through and headed across the carpet towards me and Hussein. They were not the kind of people, I will be frank, who I would normally be drawn to. The facts are stark: I have no obese or disabled friends.[2] But I did now. Boy, you should have seen the smile I flashed them as they hobbled and dipped towards me where I sat in lepers' corner with Hussein. Incredible as it may sound to you, I actually pride myself on being open minded, and able to talk to absolutely anyone, and never in my life had I been so pleased to speak to a fat, disabled woman.

I told them brightly about our trip and how well it was going while Hussein stared at me with an air of incredulity. The second woman, who had bright pink hair and big earrings, said that before she got a bad knee she'd loved walking. Now she couldn't hike any more, she drove out from Wolverhampton to look at the hills. The other lady, the fat one, was her friend. I slipped into the conversation the fact that Hussein's sister had two children with my son, who was just one of my two offspring, in an attempt to establish both my heterosexuality and consanguinity with Hussein. It made Hussein relax but I couldn't tell if the women had thought we were boyfriends. I think, for them, being in a room with a lot of walkers was probably tricky, and they, too, were trying to fit in. Maybe we all were.

'Where are you from?' The one with the walking sticks asked Hussein.

'Er, I come from Tottenham. It's my first time out here,' he said. I looked at her, trying to imagine what

[2] *You need to unpack this,* said Claude, my writer friend. What can I say? I have gone to the dentist to fix the tooth decay of racism and he has located two more infections in the root: fatism and diasbledism. Nasty abscesses. I need to tackle them before they flare up.

social political religious and racial calculations she was making. But her smile was straightforward enough.

'Do you like it?'

'Yeah, though the hills can be a bit steep.'

'But it's wonderful, the borders, a smashing part of the country,' she said. 'My favourite part of England, I'd say.'

'It's one of mine, too,' said Hussein, sweetly.

'How far you going?' one asked.

'A very long way. All the way to Llangollen,' said Hussein, making a good fist of the Welsh pronunciation.

'That's miles,' agreed the other woman.

'Forty-four,' said Hussein.

'You're very lucky. It's a fantastic trip,' said her friend with the bad knee.

The food came, and we ate together. We were a happy group, there in Rejects' Corner. The white, able-bodied normal people squeezed knee to knee at the other tables started to recede. I felt happy for Hussein, happy for the two women, and happy for myself. This had been a lesson for me. I smiled at Hussein as he picked critically at his food.

There was a catch on the door of my heart that kindness could open, which allowed my love to tumble out. I looked around at the others in the bar and thought that they, too, wanted their catch released, to let their love out.

We left the warmth of the hotel and stood in the porch where it suddenly felt chilly. I wanted a short siesta, of round about three hours, under a twenty-tog duvet in a warm room upstairs. Our boots, cold, stiff and caked in mud, were difficult to pull on. We struggled into our rucksacks and walked back round the fake castle and picked up the path with a plan to get past Montgomery, about five miles north and find a B&B on the track.

A whipping wind carved gusts of yellow leaves onto the puddles in the woods. Walking up a long field of stubble, Hussein fell a bit behind. I looked back. He made a small figure limping under a stormy grey sky.

When he caught up, he was puffed out. He did not smile.

'Problem?' I asked.

'My leg is stiff, Guy.'

'That's cramp,' I said. 'Lie down.' He sat down heavily in the field margin where the grass was quite long, 'Give me your foot,' I said and massaged his left calf.

'That hurts, Guy.'

I knelt down to press it against my shoulder, massaging some circulation back into his muscle. Right then a couple of stringy, middle-aged men who we had seen in the pub passed us. They looked like middle management, bonding while they discussed options for the business.

I glanced at them and saw them look away as they hurried past Hussein and me in the grass.

When Hussein's leg had recovered he stood up gingerly, clinging onto my arm.

'Are you going to be okay?' I asked.

'I think so. It hurts. It needs VapoRub.' **I grew up on VapoRub and paracetamol, ibuprofen if things got really bad.**

'I thought that was for chesty coughs.'

'No. It's what my leg needs.'

He hobbled for a bit and then resumed walking, though not fast.

In the next field I said, 'What do you think people think of us when they see us, apart from, you know, that?'

He tutted.

'I know you said that,' I said, 'but it's obviously not the case. I wonder what they do think? We make a fairly unlikely pair.'

'I don't know,' he said.

'Football agent and his new striker talking about which club to sign with,' I said.

He grunted.

'Or...' I continued. 'Head of geography and pupil on a field trip. The rest of the class are lagging behind.'

'That does not make sense,' he said.

'No, I agree,' I said. 'How about parole officer and ex-offender?'

'How about,' Hussein said 'OAP and his carer?'

After that, we pressed on in silence through another oak wood, whose floor bobbled with acorns. When we slipped into the back of a hamlet of no more than ten houses, and the path took us through a couple of gardens, I pulled out the map ostentatiously so it was clear we were ramblers.

An hour or two after lunch the sky clouded over and the wind whipped in some weather. Wet air borne on the Atlantic slid up the hills, slurped down into the valley and progressed across the plane shedding a blur of rain. We were in a large field with a crop of maize sewn in a rectangle at its edge.

'This is a crop for pheasant shooting,' I said. 'It's where the birds are made to hide before they're shot.'

Pacing though some admirable deciduous woods we glimpsed the pillared portico and sash windows of a large white house on a hill.

'What do you think of that?' I said, stopping to assess it, and, yes, I admit, show it off to Hussein as an example of British achievement. 'It's a big house, eh? And old.'

'Georgian,' Hussein said.

I looked at him.

'How do you know it's Georgian?' I asked.

'It's my favourite architecture, late eighteenth-century, bro,' he said.

I thought, I might as well pack this project in right now. Who is going to believe that the youth from the Tottenham council flat has a soft spot for the elegant sash windows and graceful porticos of eightieth century British buildings? I've already had to admit he's royalty.

'I would like to restore one, one day,' he smiled.

What? He was meant to be vandalising and grafittiing old buildings, not restoring them. This was getting hopeless. And to twist the knife further, he said, 'Oh, hold on. Is that an original medieval remnant on the side?'

I took a closer look and saw Hussein was right, thinking then, with a sinking heart, that I had to totally forget the textbook thug I thought I had signed up. He was sensitive and educated. He could spot original seventeenth century mullion fenestration at half a mile. What else was in his head?

'It's Mum's favourite period,' Hussein said. **I talk about my Mum so much. I never knew. Is that healthy?**[3] 'But built on slavery money,' he continued. 'The Georgian frontage.'

'I have no doubt,' said I.

[3]Yes.

'I don't think you know about colonialism, do you?'
Hussein said.

'You mean when the British kindly went to Africa to help you lot out, and give you the benefit of our civilisation and table manners?'

He walked on.

'I was joking.' I shouted after him.

He said, 'I know.'

His head was bowed as though tired, and fed up. I regretted my joke. Trying to be funny was what I did when I was feeling guilty.

It was actually quite hard to know what to say. What to do as a white Englishman about African enslavement and the profits that poured into Britain as a consequence? Support reparations. That I did.[4]

There is a department at the University of West Indies devoted to the study of Reparations for Slavery. They are basically involved with two activities: totting up the bill for slavery, i.e. the back-pay and theft of resources, and tracing the people and institutions who are the descendants of those who most benefitted, to present the account to. They don't just mean countries or races.

---

[4]*You need to unpack this* (Claude, again.) I knew some facts about reparations, and I spoke about them freely, believing all British people should talk about them. Here's one: at the end of slavery in 1832, £4 million was given to Jamaica by the British government as compensation, to the slave owners. The slaves themselves got nothing. The slaves were left to rebuild their lives, society, economy and country on the ruins of their death camps. It was as if Hitler's victims were not given a country and financial help at the end of the war, but left to scratch around in Auschwitz on their own.

They mean individual people. They have taken each slave owning plantation owner and traced their fortune and descendants to the present day. This thing: slavery, it's not something that went on just in the past, for them. It is still going in, in its effects at least, today. If one of these descendants is you, expect a mention in their literature. Expect an invoice. They are combing through colonial records, like studying Nazi records after the war, which of course were made at a time when people were not just proud but boasted of being slave owners, so the records are comprehensive.

'It wasn't very nice,' he said, and walked on. I could hear the rain pelting and blooming on his fleece. He turned and screwed up his face against a gust of wind. 'What your people did.'

'I know,' I said. 'I'm sorry.'

# 6.

The hotel we stayed at in Montgomery is a place you absolutely must stay in if you want to see how run down an underfunded, regional hotel under pressure from Airbnb and health and safety regs can get. Its decay was, to me, with my taste for decline and failure, a delight to behold, though I would not recommend a stay longer than one night. But that is all the time you need to appreciate the state of the carpet in the corridor, caked in historic grime, the extreme ugliness of the fire doors, and more particularly their placement, which satisfactorily broke up any last bits of charming space there was left in it after the calamitous refit which looked, from its frills and stripes, to have been undertaken in the mid-80s.

My bed was shoved against the radiator under the window. I had a prison TV high up on the wall which, in an era when every screen has instant access to the entire world's media, had but three channels, all of them deadly. The remote was weightless, promising and delivering nothing. A bathroom was hacked out of the corner of the tiny room and featured a cramped shower of hot needles and a labouring extractor fan.

We had agreed to meet in the bar in an hour, but after respectful appreciation of the view outside my window – a patch of mud ornamented with fag butts, a heating duct and some broken bedroom furniture – I went down to get a bit drunk. **This was my first time staying in a hotel or B&B in the UK. I thought it was ok.**

Hussein arrived in the bar when I was on my second pint. As I was bringing his Coca Cola to the table, we both noticed the two hikers who passed us earlier in the day standing in the door looking at the bar.

I moved my chair away from the table so I was looking out at the room, rather than facing Hussein, and sat down.

'Why did you move your chair?' he asked.

'To get a better look. I want to see if people are looking at us and what their expressions are. I'm doing a survey here. I'm writing a book about all of this.'

'I thought it was to get a bit further away from me.'

'No,' I answered, truthfully.

'Because did you see those two men?'

'Yes. I did. I moved to look around the room and see if people were looking at us, at you.' But the guests and staff in the hotel were cool. I felt welcomed and accepted in its horribly modernised bar and lounge area.

The following morning, at breakfast, we sat opposite each other at a small table, with the two hikers sitting opposite each other beside us. Hussein said, 'I don't want anything, Guy, I'll be up in my room,' and left.

I sympathised. Apart from anything else, I had never realised just how porky the British provincial hotel breakfast was until I considered eating one in front of a committed Muslim like Hussein. All around him, plates of bacon, pork sausage and black pudding were conveyed through the dining room and devoured off tables. Pork was a comestible which Hussein, like many people, found offensive. I loved it, but had this far resisted extolling its delights to my young friend. I thought that might cross a line with him.

After I paid the bill, I met Hussein outside the hotel and paced the three deserted streets of Montgomery looking for a place to buy VapoRub and a windcheater. I was expecting a chemist and an outdoor shop, like the one where we bought the boots, and maybe even a café to raise morale before we set off into what was looking increasingly like a wet day. We found what used to be termed a general store, the kind of place that sells everything, and was one of the first types of shops to be eviscerated by the Internet. It was a large building on three floors crammed with hardware, clothing, toys, kitchenware, like something from the 70s. A lady stood behind a worn counter in front of labelled drawers. Hussein seemed shy, so I did the talking.

'Do you have a jacket or windcheater I could buy for my friend here?'

'No, Only this. Follow me.'

She took us deep into the shop, up little flights of stairs and down a couple of steps and then round a corner past pots of paint, then up a narrow flight of stairs through a room of dog collars and cat boxes, finally to a non-descript room with a skylight over a carousel with little coloured bags dangling from it.

She unzipped one and took out a lightweight anorak.

'What colour do you want?'

He looked carefully at all the colours and chose a pale blue. He unfolded it and pulled it on. He smiled. It suited him, and fitted him. I was so relieved. It felt like the first good thing that had happened since we had started.

'Right. Let's get moving,' I said.

'But what about VapoRub, Guy?'

'Do you really need it?' I asked.

'Yes. Cos my leg is hurting, Guy.'

There wasn't a pharmacy in Montgomery, but we found a crammed corner shop with high shelves and narrow aisles. Hussein went to look for the medical shelf and I approached the woman behind the till to ask if she stocked VapoRub, but she shot past me to follow Hussein. When she returned with Hussein and the VapoRub, the woman said to me, 'Did you just put those batteries in your pocket?'

I said, 'What?'

She said, 'Did you take some batteries,' adding, 'and forget to pay?' reducing the charge from shoplifting to absent mindedness. Maybe upon hearing my plummy accent.

I said, 'Are you accusing me of shoplifting?'

She said, 'Are you buying those batteries?'

I said, 'I haven't got any batteries, and I don't want any batteries. We came in for VapoRub.'

She apologised grumpily.

I paid for the medicament and left.

'I cannot believe what just happened,' I said to Hussein on the pavement.

Hussein said nothing.

'She thought I was a shoplifter.'

Hussein seemed to look at me urgently, yet without expression.

'Oh! Oh!' I said. 'Christ. Now I see.'

Was this treatment the norm for him? He didn't either condemn it, or even apparently get angry about it. This confused me. I expect he won't even comment on this. **No I won't. I'll say what I want, when I want.** Coming on top of our treatment in the pub I wondered if this was maybe not a trip of discovery about black Britons, but white ones. We set off through the sports fields and round the sewage farm on the town's outskirts.

'We would make the perfect criminal partnership,' I said. 'You divert them and I do the crime.'

The sun came out, and the grass sparkled. A few leaves softly fell from the groves of oak, and the path was strewn with more. In a small village, we walked a pavement which we were then diverted off and sent down a side street lined with houses, and then through a garden and small orchard. I supposed that for hundreds of years the path would have brought benefit to houses it ran beside, not hazard. In an era before phones or even mail, the odd long-distance traveller would have brought fascinating and important news from far away exotic places like Bishop's Castle. Now, as far as the occupants of the houses were concerned, the path just gave strangers an excuse to lurk around the outbuildings. The ground around the trees was carpeted with apples. Many had wasp holes.

I picked one up and took a bite. 'Mmm,' I said. 'Crunchy and crisp.'

I think that's what people call my white, middle class privilege. That I could just pick up a windfall without hesitation. And it's reputed to be a thing that men like me do not notice we possess. Well, I notice it, at all times – although I agree being with Hussein had sharpened my awareness even more – and I am grateful for it. But I don't call it my privilege, I call it my basic right as a citizen of Britain. For centuries, people in Britain have fought hard so that I am able wander around the place feeling that I have some control and agency. I don't want it taken away from me, but I do want it extended to Hussein. I want that very badly, particularly seeing him glancing with furrowed brow and anxious eyes at the apples and then at me, and then the house beyond the fence. Removing my privilege was not going to give Hussein his. Removing my privilege would make it harder for Hussein to know how to act like a citizen of this country, with all the rights entailed. It annoyed me that he hesitated to pick up a windfall, because it was predicated on the idea that people would be nasty to Hussein, probably because of what he looked like. In the world that I wanted, Hussein would be confident enough to do exactly as I did. It might not be strictly within the law to pick up an apple. I have no idea and I don't care. If the owner wanted them that badly she should have come and picked them herself. No owner of an apple tree I have ever met begrudges a passer-by stooping to take a worm ridden windfall from time to time. There were scores in the long grass if you looked.

Hussein said, 'Whose are they?'

'I think if they are on the ground with some going rotten, they kind of belong to everyone by that point. It's not stealing, it's scrumping.'

'What's scrumping?'

'Scrumping is eating apples that don't belong to you. It's an old British tradition and one you need to learn about and enjoy the benefit of. Do you have any similar tradition? Where the taking of unharvested fruit goes on?'

'Yes. In Islam we call it stealing.'

'This is why I wanted to come on the walk with you!' I exclaimed. 'To show you some of our customs, help you understand and enjoy them. It's very much what makes England England.'

'Stealing fruit?'

'Stealing is something else. There's a plan involved in stealing, whereas scrumping is ad hoc. It's cheeky. It's physical banter. Does that make sense?'

'Can black people scrump? Is that the word?'

'Very good question, my friend. Of course they can. Scrumping is the inalienable right of every British citizen. But can you actually do it? Do you know how to?'

'I just pick up an apple.'

'Show me.'

Hussein glanced around him.

'No.' I said. 'It's your right, Hussein. You don't have to check if someone is looking. You conduct yourself as if they are yours by right. It's an important British habit. Take up your rights. Hold up that head, pull back those shoulders. This country's yours as much as it is anyone's. This space is yours. This path is yours to walk on.'

Hussein crouched down and started turning over the fallen apples.

'What are you doing?' I said.

'Looking for a good one.'

'Okay, but scrumping usually happens quite fast. You're not at the grocers.'

He looked at a few and picked up about three and started reaching for more.

'Scrumping is good for four bits of fruit. Beyond that it's edging towards stealing.'

I had thrown my cloak of privilege around him. We both knew it. If someone had come out of the little red brick cottage over the fence I would have protected

Hussein. He didn't say anything, and I didn't mind doing it, but I shouldn't have to do that, in a decent country.

While Hussein was inspecting his apples with apparent satisfaction and sliding them into his pockets, I said, 'Tell me, I am interested, do white people when they first meet you ever regard you with suspicion?'

'You did,' he said.

'What?' I said. 'I didn't.'

'You did. You said you had seen me looting on TV.'

'That's different. That was at a family do. You are a member of my family. I'm allowed to. I wouldn't say that to a stranger.'

'You should hear yourself sometimes,' Hussein said.

'What happened in the shop this morning, when that woman chased you around the aisle to see if you were stealing. Does that happen a lot? Are people immediately suspicious? Why didn't that make you cross?'

'That? That's nothing. I've been stopped and searched downstairs at my house in Tottenham, and I get security following me around in Westfield whenever I go in.'

'That would enrage me,' I said. 'I'd challenge them. Do you challenge them?'

'They throw you out if you do that,' Hussein said, and then he smiled, and I thought *is he picturing me being launched onto the pavement outside Westfield Shopping Centre?* **I wasn't, but I am now.**

'And I get pulled for random searches at night clubs, just the usual.'

'Just the usual? Hussein that is not usual. In all my life I have never once been searched by the police, particularly in a night club.' I was thinking of how the clientele of Annabel's would feel about being pushed up against the wall and frisked.

'I always ask myself *was it racist* after an incident, *or is it just random?*'

'It does not sound random if it has never been done to me,' I said.

'Or maybe it's just people doing their job?'

I shook my head. 'You saw what happened to us in the shop back there. That looked like racism to me. Don't you think?'

Hussein said, 'Life's more comfortable if you think not everything is race related.'

**I wouldn't say I've never experienced racism, I just try to avoid seeing things that way. I wasn't always like this, I've suspected a teacher or two in my past of being racist. I had one teacher who would just kick me out of class, or tell me my only answer should only ever be 'yes Miss or no Miss', but Mum told me to ignore all of that and keep going with my studies. And that was pretty much Mum's response every time I thought someone was being racist, 'ignore it and move on'.** With our pockets full of apples, we left the orchard through a bowered gate and took the path down the side of some scruffy fields which had the sad look of acreage that was going through a long and drawn out planning process. It was adjacent to the hamlet and was clearly not being farmed with any commitment. Its owners, probably now far away, no longer saw it as a field but as a new swimming pool, a house extension, a third car, school fees and a holiday house in the Tarn.

I was glad Hussein had no tales of being openly abused. They would have upset me. I say that, but I secretly thought that maybe he was lying, out of pride. To put himself above that nasty behaviour. No one would abuse a prince in exile. I understood that. Who wants to tell undignified stories about themselves?

I remember as a 12-year-old child seeing open abuse of a black man for the first time in my life. I was stunned, and shocked. The victim was a professional footballer at a match, probably around 1979. It was Swindon Town Football Club, at home. Somebody reading this probably knows the name of the man, because there were not many black footballers back then. All I can say is thank God there are now, or my team, Liverpool, would be struggling to avoid relegation.

When I heard the taunts of the people around me in the stand I was absolutely amazed, and wanted to shrink in size to nothing. I had been brought up by a rabidly anti-apartheid mother who lectured me and my siblings often on the iniquities of racism. Thank you, Mum, for that. She had been evacuated to South Africa during the war and had seen racial segregation close up, so she brought back a hatred for the system, which she taught me.

But I was aware as I grew up that I was to receive a different set of lessons about race than those I had heard at home. As a young teenager, I remember going to the beach with a friend and his family where they had a barbecue. My friend picked up a burnt sausage and called it Neddy N-word, and everyone except me laughed. My face smarted because I knew it to be shameful behaviour. But none of them noticed me. And I thought maybe my Mum had got it wrong. It wouldn't be the first time. She also filled my head with an idea that I was an aristocrat, despite her father being a shopkeeper.

Hussein and I met a woman walking her dog in a second tussocky, almost thicketed, field. The dog was a little terrier who was barely visible in the long grass. You could just see the grasses moving above him. We stopped to talk to her; she too had been a big walker until her knees went. She said she saw hundreds of people on the path, as she lived beside it, nodding towards a modern house beyond a wooden fence. She asked where we were from and where we were going. We were getting quite used to these Offa's Dyke conversations.

When she had turned back with her terrier, Hussein stopped to apply the VapoRub. He wanted to put it on his calves, but his jeans were too tight at the ankle to roll up. He needed to take his trousers down to do the job properly. I stood off eating my apple, which I saw now was rotten, while he looked for a secluded spot against a big hedge. He nearly toppled over while balancing with his trousers down so I went to give him a steadying hand. I was looking to see if he had applied the VapoRub to all the affected area when I heard a click, and saw the two walkers who we had last seen at breakfast standing at the gate, staring at us. They walked past us in silence as Hussein tried to pull up his trousers.

# 7.

The day grew hotter, the sky clearer, the sun harsher. The hills became tough work. I kept looking at the map thinking, *that can't be right.*

Hussein said, 'Is this turning out to be harder than you thought, Guy?'

'It's all part of the adventure,' I replied.

'Have you ever heard of heatstroke?' he asked.

I ignored him, setting the pace ahead.

'Only you can die of it,' I heard him say under his breath.

The path was now revealing a certain inflexible side to Offa's character. Standing at the base of a steep knoll I complained to Hussein that Offa could perfectly well have told his men to go round the bottom of the hillock, but instead directed his dyke masters to take the path straight up over it and down the other side. Offa, to a builder, was the client from hell. There were no short cuts. It was a manifestation of his power, and Hussein and I were now his victims. Hussein looked frankly miserable, and was not apparently cheered up by me saying, 'Don't worry, this struggle will make it all the more rewarding when we reach our destination.'

'But we've only done 12 miles, and we got 28 to go. How long's it gonna take us?'

'Come on, keep going.'

We got out of the sunlight and into the shade of some commercial forestry. The track had been widened by the owners so the industrial timber machines could get to the harvest. I spotted some bogus signs trying to put off walkers: KEEP OUT. BIRD BREEDING AREA. The only birds allowed to breed in that wood were commercial pheasants. As we went deeper into the compartment[1] I noticed we were walking over the ivy-clogged foundations of sunken Victorian brickwork: a house, a bridge, a damn, a terrace of sheds and a drained pond where poults were being raised. We were on the ruins of a huge, rich estate that had been run into the ground over a period of about fifty years, maybe longer.

There are few things in rural Britain uglier than raising pheasants. Blue barrels, filthy troughs, muddy ground, rusty fencing and rotten posts, all possessed the air of something on its last legs, literally in the case of the birds.

The rights of the walkers could never be superseded by a pheasant breeder's. The signs were unlawful, bullying. I wondered if timid people turned back thinking it was some kind of sanctuary, where rare birds were nesting. All around was the casual vandalism of an out-of-control gamekeeper. Empty bags of feed pinned against a fence, lengths of discarded blue pipe, and rusting feeders blown over on the charnel ground in the pens.

[1]Claude: What's a compartment? Answer: It's a technical term for an area of commercial woodland.

I hoped a keeper would appear on his ATV and try to intimidate me so I could give him a piece of my mind. Particularly as Hussein was watching. By watching me practise my privilege he could maybe learn the trick. It wasn't that difficult, you just said what you thought. And showed clearly that you respected all people and feared none.

Apart from the young pheasants, which rustled in the shadows like huge cockroaches, and the tiny trickles of surface water on the track, the forest was silent. My breathing became heavier as the long, straight hill steepened. Hussein started getting left behind but I thought I would continue to the top and wait for him in a conversion spot.[2] Behind the pheasant wire the miserable trees looked like prisoners in a POW camp. Skeletal and diseased, they were a long way from teak counter tops, fine furniture and handsome floor boards. The trees felt apologetic, crowded together, anaemic, scrofulous, and quite unlike the old oaks we had walked under earlier. They were man's work, not nature's.

I looked back again, and Hussein had stopped in the middle of the track. He was massaging his leg. He looked up, saw me and pushed on, like a mountaineer in the death zone on Everest. One heavy foot after another, exhausted. I didn't know that he had been in agony all morning, but hiding it from me. I guess he didn't want to let me down, or spoil the project. I sat on a butt of

---

[2]Another commercial woodland term meaning a place where the trunks are stacked and loaded onto trucks for transport to the saw mill to be made, in the case of these trees, into medium density fibre board, fence posts and flimsy roof lathes.

a tree and stared at the wood chips in the oily puddles while Hussein toiled up the hill. He limped onto the flat.

'Take a rest. You need a rest,' I said.

He grimaced as he took off his rucksack and sat down. I silently calculated the time it would take us to complete the walk at this speed: about three weeks.

'Take off your boot, let's have a look.'

'It's the back of my leg. It hurts.'

I couldn't feel any swelling. He stood up on one leg, and when he took a step with the other he screwed up his face. We were a long way from a road. He looked up the track disappearing into the forest and I thought I saw tears in his eyes.

'I don't think I can go on, Guy.'

The walk was meant to have been a delightful unfolding of the joys of the British countryside and an extended conversation about the glories of being British, but had ended up with him hobbling across an ugly conversion spot in a commercial forestry compartment, barely able to talk to me.

'We'd better keep moving,' I said, 'there's a road ahead.'

He hobbled painfully behind me to the road where we sat on a metal car barrier by the fire spot of a burnt-out car.

'I, I can't go further, man.' Hussein said. 'There's something wrong. I've got an issue with my leg.'

This had not gone as planned. He looked miserable. It felt like the ground we had walked over had somehow attacked Hussein. The past had risen through the soil to manacle him. The rich men who built this estate, no doubt, yes, with pillaged and bloody money, though superseded by generations of increasingly poorer and probably more decent descendants, would not release the black man from their land. The past would not let go. It was present with Hussein and me.

I put my arm around his shoulder and tried to help him like walking a soldier off the battlefield but he said it was easier on his own. I walked beside him as he shuffled his way down a public road that sloped steeply down to Welshpool, which we could see about four miles away on the valley floor. We left the footpath and limped into town, Hussein going slower and slower until finally he sat on the verge and said, 'I can't stand up, Guy. I can't walk.'

There was a school playground that suddenly filled with kids on a break; some of them came to the wire and stared at Hussein and me, before being led away by a teaching assistant. I tried to give Hussein a hand up but he said, 'It's no good. I can't stand. I need an Uber.'

I got out my phone, found a local taxi company and did my best to explain where we were. Half an hour later a car drew up slowly with a young woman at the wheel, staring at Hussein.

'We need to get to the train station.'

Hussein got in and we drove across the valley into town. The grand Victorian station had been closed down and sold off as a café and an outlet for factory seconds. The active part of the station was now a vending machine on a platform about 500 yards from the old ticket office and waiting room.

Hussein sat at a pub table outside the shop; he was in a bad way, and laid his head on his folded arms. He had put his fleece and windcheater in a plastic bag whose stretched handle looked as near to breaking point as Hussein. I went in to try and find some food. When I came out, I thought how like a refugee he looked. Or like the ones I saw on TV and also used to glimpse on the hard shoulder on the autoroute near Calais. The ones who had come from Sudan, on foot. I touched him on the shoulder and offered him some wine gums, then wondered if they contained some kind of pork product.

'We have to go over the footbridge to get to the platform,' I said.

He groaned.

'Come on, I'll help you.'

I tugged him onto his feet, put my arm round his waist and told him to put his arm round my neck. He hobbled beside me in step. As we passed a café, the door opened and out came two men who looked familiar.

'Look who it is,' Hussein whispered. It was the men from the hotel who saw Hussein with his trousers down by the orchard. **I hope those two find this book and read it.**

I held onto Hussein and smiled weakly. They looked away quickly and pretended they hadn't seen us.

'At least we look very much in love,' Hussein said.

I laughed.

'And you are not just you paying me for sex. You know?'

¯\_(ツ)_/¯

**(I got an emoji in)**

# 8.

One symptom of Hussein's mental condition was that he couldn't travel on trains. He told me he had vomited on nearly every platform of the Circle line. I had asked him if he could put into words what he was anxious about.

He said, 'Well, it's difficult to describe. I have been in therapy for it. The NHS doctor recommended me. It's like, it's like I feel overwhelmed by an event coming towards me.'

'Something huge?' I asked.

'Yes, Guy, that is what I am saying.'

'Like bad?' I said.

'No. Something so exciting I can't deal with it.'

'What?' I said, 'You are anxious about something going really well?'

'Yes, Guy,' he said miserably. 'No one understands that.'

'I do, I do, my friend. All these anxieties are fiendish, I understand. And I'll try to keep you safe. Look, let's stay the night in Welshpool and see how we feel in the morning.'

'No Guy, I must go home.'

'To Tottenham?'

'Yes. Can you call me a taxi?'

'To Tottenham?'

'Or to your friend in Llangollen.'

'But that's the end of the walk then?'

'I want to go in a taxi, not a train.'

When Hussein had told me he was a prince, it was a young Henry V I had in my mind. Prince Hal. I was obviously his Falstaff. On the course of our walk, with my guidance, I would see him turn from the boy prince into the man king. But with his extravagant transport demands he was beginning to remind me of another prince altogether: Prince Andrew.

I got Hussein to agree to a short train journey and a taxi to a friend's house where we could stay the night. The next day I would get my car and drive him back to London. He was done in. We boarded the train, and as it was almost full, we had to sit apart, though Hussein chose to crouch with his head in his hands in the space for baggage, next to a guy with a bike.

'Are you okay?' I asked when we drew off.

'No,' he groaned.

I tried to reassure him that he would be okay. I didn't ask him what he was scared might happen. It certainly didn't look like he was being overwhelmed by the thought of an exciting event.

I sat opposite a woman who picked up some food in front of her three-year-old and said, 'Have you finished your cheese?' as she put it in her own mouth.

We rattled through the border landscape at a truly unfamiliar speed after being used to walking. I kept looking back at Hussein to check he was okay, or at least that he wasn't in serious peril. He looked scared and miserable.

I suspected that this was the end of the mission. I had failed. The project to help Hussein recover his mojo had fallen flat on its face. The love affair I had promoted between Hussein and the British countryside had fizzled out before it got started.

The gap seemed too impossibly wide. And as for the improvement in his mental health, that wasn't too impressive, either.

# 9.

The winter swept in, surprisingly, almost alarmingly, warm and wet, and as I wrote up the chapters I was pleased to be working on a topic more crucial than global warming. After all, what was the point of survival of the species if we humans persisted in hating one another?

I stayed at my home in Somerset to write, listening to droplets of rain scratching at my windows. The Windrush scandal and Brexit dominated the news, both of which made life embarrassing for middle-aged white blokes like me, no matter how unracist I actually was, because it turned out I was well in the frame for both.[1]

Not just because I have spent many happy months of my life in Jamaica, and possess many close Jamaican

---

[1]Unpack this. (Claude. Of course. He always wants me to dig deeper, and do more work, thank goodness. While he sips wine and criticises.) The winter of 2019 was a time of heightened racial and political tensions in the UK. Brexit was perceived as a racist enterprise advanced mainly by middle-aged whites. And the outrageous treatment of the Caribbean people who came to live in the UK after the war was also perceived at least to have been done in the name of the same middle-aged white people.

friends, the Windrush scandal made me twitch and seethe with fury. My whole pitch to Hussein about the delights of being British was predicated on the idea that there were not two classes of Briton. There was just us. One lot. No matter our creed, sexual orientation or colour we stood shoulder to shoulder as equals. So, when the Windrush affair proved the exact opposite, I was outraged and ashamed.

The Home Office's protestations that it was hard to identify people who had lived in Britain for 40 years were despicable. I could have established in a twenty-minute conversation with anyone whether or not they had been in Britain for the last twenty-five years. It would be a doddle. Who was Roland Rat? What school did you go to? What was your head called? What school did Zammo McGuire go to? Where in London is the carnival? Job done. One correct answer gets full UK citizenship and a big apology. How difficult was it for the Home Office to do that?

I was already red in the face (or redder than usual) and spluttering on my whisky and soda whenever I thought about Amber Rudd, the Home Secretary. I had been at university with her and had even directed her in *The Sound of Music*. She had been cast as the Baroness, who hated the Nazis, if I remember the plot correctly. What really sent me over the edge with incoherent fury was that in some way these decisions were being made in my name, or with my implicit approval, just because I looked like an ageing, racist relic. As a middle class, middle-aged white man, it was done in my name, but without my permission. It maddened me that the tiny minds at Conservative HQ thought just because I was right wing economically, I was also a racist. How have the two not been separated? I resent it. It is hell being black in a racist world, but it isn't much fun being white, either. That was why I was on a walk in the middle of nowhere with Hussein.

I sent the manuscript off to Hussein for his notes. While I was waiting for him to return it, I spoke to a few friends about this project and most were bewildered when I told them it had started off as a book about nationality, friendship and family and had quickly descended into a book that questioned my own racism.

'Good luck with that,' one of my close mates said.

Another friend said, 'Young black dude and an old white man? Have you thought about TV? Is he good looking?'

My friend Nick Quinn, a film director who lived in Paris, was interested enough to come to London and shoot a test with me and Hussein. The idea was that we might make a TV couple, Hussein and I. Like The Hairy Bikers. Our journey would no longer be this book, but a TV serial. *Footnotes with Guy and Hussein*. Six half-hour episodes. BBC. They might call it *The Journey*. Mic'd up, we would walk the footpaths of Britain talking about this and that and bump into colourful local characters the producer had set up for us. **Actually sounds nice, the idea in my head was more Bear Grylls out in the wild, foraging for berries, using local farms shops for food and camping out at night while the cameras are on, and as soon as they turn off the crew picks us up and drives us to the nearest 5 star hotel.** I imagined the future: not the tedious hours of re-walking fields and going over stiles four times to get all the angles for the camera, which is the truth of reality TV, but an immediate and effortless fame. Hussein and Guy. Hussein and I. Me and Hussein, media stars. **I'm surprised you didn't call it Me and Me (with Hussein)**

Here we are at the launch of the series, being interviewed by a rapt press corps. Hussein, beaming with the innocent joy of early celebrity, my brow knit as I fielded the more intellectual inquiries. An irresistible partnership. So unusual, so charming, so successful. I saw a coffee table book, with colour photos of me and Hussein on coastal paths, canal pubs and bridges over rivers. A Radio 4 series would be an add on. *Hussein and Guy sail the Nile, Cross the Sahara, Tackle the Rift Valley. Hussein and Guy in the USA. Hussein and Guy do South America. On the Silk Road with Hussein and Guy. Ten megacities with Hussein and Guy.* There wasn't a gig we couldn't handle. We would end up with *Hussein and Guy's Earth.* **In my head all of this sounds nice – I know I'd hate the fame part but would love the travelling and the money.**[2] And part of the TV fantasy was propelling Hussein to stardom. Because I would love his voice to be heard. There weren't any people on TV like Hussein; he was so unpushy, so humble, living life in that cramped flat with the kids clambering all over him, refreshingly unlike the folk who usually barge in front of a TV camera. When you trained a lens on someone you immediately brought out the worst in them. Or that was how it worked with me.

It was blustery and cold but sunny the day I met with Nick, the film director, in Tottenham. Litter skidded across the pavement and a plastic bag rose in a mini whirlwind as Nick did up his jacket. I called Hussein

[2]Hussein, I love you so much.

down on the intercom, because I thought it was easier than going up. Whereas I was all charm and jokes with Nick, a burly, shrugging Parisian, Hussein, when he appeared, was exactly his surly cynical self. He looked neither interested in, nor wary of, the camera. He maintained his usual air of reserving judgement for another time. When it was probably going to be pretty bad.

It was decided that we would film Hussein and me walking in a rural setting, engaging in light banter about racism, nationalism and identity politics. Hussein said he knew where a bit of countryside was, so we climbed in the car and drove under some fly-overs and through a deserted industrial estate with a lot of dirty caravans on the kerb, to a car park next to a canal with a metal portal to stop vans parking. We drew up next to a man sitting in his car smoking a fag.

As Nick took his equipment out the bag and looked at the dials, I felt myself metamorphosing into a weapons-grade TV wanker: I checked my appearance in a reflection, I arranged my hair, I adjusted my collar, I think I even coughed to clear my throat. Then I watched Hussein prepare for the filming. He did none of the above, **I think I did comb my hair that day, something I usually don't do if I'm around white people because most don't notice the difference,** and was wired for sound as though he had radio mics threaded through his shirt every day. Then he hung about without checking his appearance once. Instead, he got out his phone and started streaming the Arsenal game, totally cool.

We were in the Lea Valley; Hussein had often told me how great the park was, and how he used to go there as a kid to run around, but you could see lorries through the leafless trees and hear the rumble of traffic. I was hoping he would acknowledge the superiority of the Welsh borders, but he seemed proud and happy of his litter-spotted valley with its inert canal. **There's some really nice parts of Lea Valley park, with views into the city.** On one of the barges, a man in a thick coat sat amongst some pot plants smoking. Beyond him I saw a block of flats, a pylon, a crane and acres of warehouse. A disenchanted white bird mooched around a neglected river cruiser.

Still, I was happy, thinking this TV caper would relieve me of having to do any actual writing, and possibly any more long-distance walking. I had read that Bear Grylls filmed his journeys into the wilderness from the comfort of a luxury hotel, being convoyed out to certain spots along the way to do the shot and be back in the bar for a steak by nightfall. **Looks like me and Guy read the same tabloids.** If we were making a TV programme, bugger this book. It wouldn't need to be finished. Who would want that when there was a box set of my flippant yet undeniably incisive musings? And if they did want the book, we could employ some hack to impersonate me on the page. Job done. **I have always said there's no need to read a book, because all the good ones get turned into films or tv series.**[3]

With these warming thoughts in mind, I was keen that Hussein and I should make a good impression.

We walked along the tarmac path with Nick running backwards just in front of us with the camera, and then turned round and did it in the other direction. The idea

[3]Sacrilege. See me after class.

was that it would look like the Offa's Dyke footpath, but it so obviously didn't. One glaring problem was the other walkers: they just weren't Offa's Dyke people. This lot stared at their phones waiting for their dogs to poo, glancing round to see if they had to pick it up, before heading back to the car park. They were in white trainers and had no maps on lanyards. They shivered with their arms around themselves. Quite a few had a high BMI and would have trouble squeezing through the kissing gates.

Conversation between me and Hussein was at first stilted, but after half an hour we got one good take in which we chatted about Islam and terrorism, that old chestnut, though it still felt fake to me. He naturally pooh-poohed the idea that militants were trying to radicalise him, and told the story of how bothersome MI5 was, always pestering his community for intel.

Hussein was a TV natural. He never looked at the camera, in fact he acted as if it wasn't there, at one point getting out his phone to check the Arsenal score while I was talking. **I was nervous AF hence the Arsenal game on my phone.** I went all Raymond Burke doing an in-depth piece for Panorama about the Muslim youth of today. I said things like, 'So would you say there's any pressure on young Muslims to get into gangs, or radicalise?' (Answer: for the third time, no.) He declined to expand, clearly enjoying my discomfort, as I didn't have a follow up question ready. At one point I thought he was suppressing a smile or even outright laughter. Quite how we had got into interview mode I didn't understand, maybe it was because Hussein had sensibly fallen silent, sensing the stupidity of the TV project, and the indignity of our position, which was increased when the director looked at the material and said, 'Damn, I forgot to turn on the sound. I'm afraid we're going to have to do it again.' And Hussein and I walked back up to the beginning and made a really poor stab at repeating the stilted conversation that we had already had.

We got back in the car; it was nice to be out of the raw, metallic wind. I said, 'I think that went quite well'.

Neither the director nor Hussein said anything, but the a few days later Nick called saying he didn't think it worked. The chemistry or even the concept was missing something on film.

I broke the news to Hussein, who seemed unconcerned. I was disappointed because I wanted Hussein to enjoy some notoriety in the public eye. *Hussein and Guy's Planet Earth* – a twenty-four-part series, was obviously not to be.

# 10.

For one reason or another, a full year elapsed, which meant we were hiking through autumn again in 2019. We planned to start at the same Offa's Dyke way marker that we had staggered down the hill a year ago to find a taxi to Welshpool.

I picked Hussein up in Tottenham, as once again he was unable to get on public transport. Always thin, he had lost more weight and seemed more than usually nervy, though it didn't stop him tutting at some junkies in the stairwell.

Driving through sludgy traffic on the North Circular, I was unable to wipe some smears off my windscreen.

'Looks like you forgot to fill the washer,' Hussein said, helpfully.

I refused to buy a plastic flagon of screen wash for about five reasons, the chief of which was I was not going to pay five pounds for something which was virtually free from the tap. I had meant to pour a jug in before I set off but my mind had been other things. Instead of explaining this, because I feared Hussein's judgement, I pretended I could see through the dirt.

'Isn't it illegal to drive with limited vision?' Hussein said. 'According to the Highway Code?'

Before we got to my house we stopped for fish and chips in a crowded shop in Somerset because I didn't want to cook. **I was looking forward to the fish and chips, Guy told me they were voted as being one of the best fish and chips in Britain. I thought they were meh.**[1] Everybody gawped at Hussein. He stood still, smiling at nothing, to signal general kindness and humility, it looked to me.

When we were back in the car I said, 'They all stared at you. Being black in rural Britain is like being famous.'

'Except no one wants a selfie with me.'

At my house, Hussein fell silent and seemed distant and fearful. As I packed my rucksack, he sat on the floor leaning against the Aga, consumed by his phone screen. **I sat by the Aga and near enough always sit by the Aga whenever I get to the house. Guy's house is either always cold or I'm just used to living in a much warmer house.** I was coming to the conclusion that he must have been having a hard time since we last met.

'Anxiety level?' I asked.

'No less than 4, Guy,' he said. 'Maybe 5.'

I looked at my overstuffed rucksack **Guy also found his beloved head torch in the rucksack, after years of accusing a mate of not returning it.** I suffered from the condition of over-packing luggage at the best of times, and tended at the last minute to squeeze stupid things in which, at the other end, were never needed. I once took spare fuses and a nutcracker on holiday. Glancing

[1] Never a good word for our British traditions.

at Hussein I found myself picking up a tape measure wondering if it might be wise to have it on board. Might I want to know the height of a stile? Probably not. I put it back on the table.

With one thing and another, the next day we left my house late and didn't get into our starting position on the mountain above Welshpool until about three in the afternoon.

I turned off the engine and we sat and looked through the windscreen at the Offa's Dyke oak leaf etched into the post without moving. This was because it was an established fact that the most tortuous yards of a 40-mile walk were the first ten. I scratched my ankle. I had a flare up of psoriasis on my legs. A good walk would improve that. Walking improved everything except blisters, in my book. And this is my book.[2] With each mile of walking I earned credit that I could spend on drinking, eating and lazing around at home. My flaky skin was telling me I was in overdraft.

It was warm in the car and looked chilly outside. As soon as we got going, we'd both start feeling better. But neither of us moved. I looked across at him, hunched up, lost and miserable. It was no longer Prince Andrew. It was all looking a bit Prince Edward.

Walking to improve health is a relatively recent activity in Britain. When I was a child in the 60s absolutely no one walked by choice, except for a few wiry ramblers

[2]At that point I had not really given a lot of thought to the billing on the cover of this book. I figured as it was my idea and I was doing most of the writing, the sole credit should be mine, though it did slightly raise questions in the back of my mind about how fair that was to Hussein.

who were considered as cranky as vegetarians. It was a sign something was wrong if you had to walk in 1972. But being puny and wheezy unfortunately stopped being a sign of intelligence in the 1980s, unless you were in the Ramones. Even I took up walking, in a modest way, by the 90s, after noticing that I returned from a hike in a much better mood than I set off on one. And the further I walked the happier I felt. By the millennium, any connection walking had once had with poverty and manual labour was severed, and I could lecture anyone who listened on the many and diverse benefits of walking, often from my sofa with a glass of wine in my hand. After establishing that my audience had not read *The Songlines* by Bruce Chatwin, a masterly book about moving on foot through a landscape published in 1986, I airily passed off his ideas as my own. I fascinated people with my (i.e. his) thesis that there was an aesthetic, spiritual and anthropological dimension to walking. One of the reasons walking was so soothing was that the rhythm reminded us of our mother's heartbeat when we were safely in her womb. **Didn't know about that, but I did learn from a *Family Guy* episode about runners high, which I'm guessing is similar but less to do with mums and more to do with chemicals in the brains.**

After prescribing a good long walk for the whole country, a hitch developed. I got very good at planning and talking about expeditions, but less proficient at actually going on them. That was when I learnt that it was actually the first ten yards of any walk that were torture. It was as if they had to be tackled dragging the sofa behind me, and that was utterly pointless because it would never get through the back door. Better to give up. Do it tomorrow. Before I could even find my boots, I was weighed down by reasons not to go out: the rain, the heat, the snow, the sleet, the sweat, the joint pain, the thirst, the logs, the sheaf of admin, the next chapter, a phone call, these and much more told me to delay my walk, or better still cancel it.

Hussein looked as though a variation of this was going through his mind too. The car was pulled up on a triangle of long grass facing the post that said OFFA'S DYKE FOOTPATH in both directions. Neither of us moved. We were in a place of pain. Literally, for Hussein. It was here, a year ago, we had admitted defeat, and the memory of it was sharp **I was looking up at the steep climb ahead**. I was about to tell him how good he'd soon be feeling when we got going, but something made me hesitate, I guess fear of Hussein actually bursting into tears.

'Come on,' I said. 'You'll be okay.'

I opened my door and let in some sharp autumn air. Late afternoon sun filtered into the forestry compartment, gilding conifer trunks deep in the gloom.

Hussein got out of the car and shivered. I unfurled the map and sized up the first section of our walk: an unrelenting climb up the edge of the wood and then beside a hedge, to the top of a hill, where an ancient earthworks and a monument of some kind stood, the name of which I could only read if I found my glasses which would require searching seven pockets so I didn't bother.

'Have you got on enough clothes?' I said, folding the map.

'I should be all right.' He zipped a light jacket up to his neck, making him look like he was nipping out for a pint of milk, not embarking on a 25-mile hike.

We tore ourselves away from the car and I pushed on ahead in the fringe of the wood, on packed rubble and pine needles, beside a droopy fence. I didn't talk; I wanted to get some serious walking done first, to show intent, which I feared was lacking in Hussein. It was a long climb, straight enough for me to see the path stretch out to the copse on the top of the hill. The slight insecurity about direction that had set in after ten minutes was eased by the sight of a well-built kissing gate with vertical posts and galvanised hinges amongst all the bent and rusty fencing.

I thought about the gate as I pressed on. It was set so carefully and worked so smoothly, the gate gently falling back and not banging on to the lower post, that I suspected it was the work of volunteers, probably under the supervision of some kind of countryside officer who'd completed a course and attended a good few seminars in field craft. I thought it was the work of volunteers because the job had obviously not been done in haste, the way the slack rusty barbed wire had been stapled to the hawthorn tree further up the track. I imagined a farmer effing and blinding at a bunch of escapee Welsh mountain sheep **I still think its pretty amazing that this footpath goes through people's front and back gardens as well as working farms** as the hail rattled on his back while he felt for the staples in his pocket. At walking pace there was time for these thoughts. On foot I received information at the speed I could fully process it. Maybe that was one of the reasons my mind felt so fresh after a walk. It had not had to deal with that surfeit of stimulation which came with a modern life.

I had a habit, when I lived in London, of looking into houses at dusk during my walks along its shiny streets. I didn't need to stop and stare, though occasionally I was hurried on by a woman drawing the curtains making problematic eye contact. Each window was a vignette to embroider and enjoy: a child leaning over homework at a dining room table; a book-lined sitting-room with the TV on; an unmade bed through a dirty basement window.

When I moved to Wales, I learnt the new landscape walking its lanes, tracks and paths. On foot, my senses burst into life: I felt the weight of the wind, its direction and temperature, I caught the dank and sweet smell of the ditches and woods, and I heard the screeching buzzards and distant grumbling tractors. Travelling by car my senses were hooded, and in a plane, suffocated.

For the past decade I have lived near Glastonbury, and most days I pounded off anxiety going up and down the Glastonbury Tor. The idea that walking was an anti-depressant, something which would have been laughable in the 70s, is now fairly standard. The climb up the Tor was the same as fifty flights of stairs. I got to know the Tor's steep concrete and wood steps individually. I knew, for instance, which one marked the most painful part of the walk, after which the climb levelled out. I observed that people on their way up the Tor were often out of sorts and argumentative, usually after a car ride, and because the prospect of the walk was miserable, but when they got back down from the top they were without exception (and I looked for one) happy, playful and romantic. The steep walk got the oxygen cantering around our bodies, scattering grumpy thoughts and welcoming in joyful ones. At the top of the hill you got a breath-taking panorama of the Somerset Levels, that is, if you had any breath left. The experience mocked the tiny, scentless world of the Internet. I came down shriven, healed, full of optimism and possibility.

I stopped to watch Hussein negotiate what should be renamed, from the way he went through it, the scowling-gate. Then I looked up the path, no longer of old stone but now wet grass that flopped over in bunches. I liked the way the character and mood of the path changed at gates and breaks, usually because a new arrangement with the grazing animals was established. I could see the sun on the wide fields up ahead. The hedge was bitten and scragged by years of hungry sheep.

I fell into my stride and I hit my rhythm, calculating how much to shorten my step so I didn't need to slow down before I reached the top. When a path was flat and easy, I gazed around me at the landscape and weather, but when a hill brought sweat out between my shoulder blades, like this one did, I dropped my head and stared at the ground, focussing on putting one boot in front of the other. I was wearing hand-tooled, bull hide walking boots with laces pulled through seven pairs of eyes. I had had them specially made for me. Like my expensive handmade suits, they didn't fit particularly well. I got them from John Lobb, a high-end shoemaker in St James, an exclusive part of London. The boots cost £800, a long time ago, which in today's money, adjusted for inflation, is a fucking ridiculous amount for a pair of shoes. **Guy's just promised me two pairs when the** book does well[3] I was measured for them by a young man with black skin and dreadlocks. First, he made my last.[4] His presence in that shop, taking into account the date and the extreme conservativeness of the business, was unusual.

The dreadlocked man in Lobb's had looked like what we used to call a 'token black guy'. I don't use that term (except in quotation marks) any more. The phrase was meant to criticise the white people who controlled the narrative into which the 'token' black person was inserted, but I had begun to think that it denigrated the black woman or man just as much. **It assumes the black person has no skills to merit his/her position, and I'd think no business is crazy enough to pay someone to be on display.**

If employing the young man and putting him on show in the shop was an attempt to court popularity by pretending to customers that everything at John Lobb's, which proudly boasted the Royal Warrant, was racially harmonious, the owners may have made a miscalculation. The crusty old aristos and arrogant young turks[5] who were shod there would more likely have been alarmed at the sight of a dread handling their footwear than impressed.

Most likely he was just a great shoemaker. **Black kids get told to work twice as hard, and my first thought would have been how hard did he have to work to get**

[3]I think that Hussein's remark is part of a larger negotiation about writing credits and royalties.
[4]The last is the object a shoemaker makes the shoe around.
[5]Turk is slang for arrogant young business man. I don't think it's racist, but I suspect it soon will be.

there, but on the other side there's some white people who probably think there's black people getting jobs they don't deserve just to be on display as a token whatever. And he made my boots. Pity they didn't fit. Or rather they didn't fit for the first five years. To his credit they fit snugly now, as they took me up the hill, after wearing them in for a mere twenty years. **Notice the black man's foresight, thinking twenty years ahead.**

I now considered the boots my friends. They were a couple I knew. I liked to go rambling with them. A quiet pair, but good listeners. And when we weren't walking, they hung around at my place. I hardly ever saw one without the other. Joined at the hip, they were. Though there was once a puppy that they occasionally went out with alone. Otherwise, inseparable. They looked damn good for their age, but so would you if you moisturised with dubbin.

I stopped to check where we were while Hussein caught up, looking for the grimy fold on the ordnance survey map we had reached last year. I glanced at the wooded hills and half expected to see a big brown bund which was the crease in the map.

It took about an hour to plod to the top of the hill, where a sun-faded sign about the hill fort stood behind a bench which we sat on to look at the fifty mile view: to our right the dark and empty mountains of Wales and to our left the village-speckled plain of England. I took a good photograph of Hussein, but he wasn't interested in looking at it. **I hate taking pictures. It's a constant source of anxiety and reminders of what was, is and could have been. At home, Mum has a picture of me back when I was ten-years-old wearing a badly fitted tux, paired up with a Red Sox cap and my big old ears flopping about,** with my teeth on display as I attempted to smile. At the time I seriously thought I was a young hybrid of James Bond and someone like Thierry Henry. But looking at it now, I cringe and almost certainly come close to tearing up as my sister and everyone else in the room starts laughing at how ridiculous I looked. And then I start thinking about the aspirations I had then, finish school, go to sixth form (Wood House) get 4 A*, get to uni and not any uni but Oxford, to study law, and become a barrister. And if that didn't work out the back up was to become a politician. And looking at that picture basically reminds me of how big my dreams were.[6]

I left him to brood while I looked around for the engraved oak leaf. About twenty years ago someone had planted fir trees in a clear attempt to conceal the prehistoric earthworks from the public. And someone more recently had removed the footpath signs, in an attempt to confuse people coming up here for a look around. I poked about for some clues and found the snapped post engraved with an oak leaf shoved in the hedge. It looked, from the overgrown brambles, as if it had been there a year or two. Was it the work of the same man? Had his campaign to deter British people from seeing their birth right really been going on for thirty years? Or was the broken waymarker the work of another person? His son! His heir! Who, as the new owner of the estate, was carrying on his father's visionary work to deter the public? The wily old estate manager would have spotted the sign in the hedge – nothing

[6]You've got to keep dreaming Hussein. It is all ahead of you. All to play for. You can achieve anything if you work for it.

escaped his eye – and smiled approvingly. The young master *was* his father's son. There had been dangerous talk of going organic, supporting the right to roam and breaking into eco-tourism when the boy first inherited, but the manager and the gamekeeper had taken the lad into the gun room and explained to him that that sort of nonsense was for lesser estates. This was a British shooting estate and it would not demean itself like Longleat with its queues of families having a fun day out. Families were not meant to have a fun day out on privately owned British farmland. They were meant to feel unwelcome. I smiled at the vignette which had blossomed in my imagination from the climb up the hill.

'Don't you feel wonderful now?' I shouted to Hussein.

He zipped up his jacket to his chin. 'I feel cold, Guy,' he said.

I located a wide ride through the anaemic Sitka spruce. Here and there you could see the undulations of the ancient fort.

'Spooky,' Hussein said. 'I don't like it.'

I didn't like it either, because of its mean spirit. This site should have been celebrated as a venerable and ancient human settlement. Who knew, maybe even Offa himself had passed through and spent the night, while looking for the steepest hill to build his dyke over. **If Offa himself had to walk this footpath there wouldn't be as many steep climbs.**

The track in the wood mysteriously narrowed and then stopped abruptly at a wall of pines which we had to duck and weave through towards the light while being jabbed by pointy branches. We struggled to the edge of the wood and stood in a bog, rubbing pine dust from our eyes and inspecting our clothes for tears. Our way was now barred by a ditch full of black water with a rusty fence on the other side and no sign of any stile. We scrambled down and up the ditch, and helped each other over the fence. The Offa's Dyke was meant to be the M6 of footpaths but here was Hussein wobbling on a bit of pig netting while daintily taking my hand to help him jump the barbed wire into a random field.

'That land owner should be reported,' I said. 'It's not British to obstruct rights of way. That's what you should expect when you are British, Hussein: the right to walk your beautiful country free of let and hindrance. It's the Queen's highway. It's your birth right as a Briton. I bet it's not like that in Somalia.'

'It's Sharia law there, Guy. If you went walking in Somalia, they would probably kidnap, torture and kill you,' he said.

'That's quite an extreme public access policy,' I said.

'I expect your man here would approve,' Hussein replied. 'I think quite a lot of English landowners would like that,' he added.

We were looking at a long and wide field whose gentle curve had a welcoming softness after the stabbing we got in the wood. The sheep had nibbled the turf down to a green fitted carpet. But there was no sign of any path across it.

I had bought a plastic-bound route map booklet of the Offa's Dyke Path that was easier to handle than the squeezebox map, so I handed it to Hussein and said, 'What do you reckon?'

He looked up from the page of the booklet and scanned the meadow ahead of us. Further up the hill a flood had filled a dip with water and half submerged a galvanised gate. 'It's not there, is it?' I said.

'No,' Hussein said, pointing to a hedge about quarter of a mile away. 'There.'

Sure enough, I could just see a stile under a ragged old hawthorn bearing a yellow mark, which as we drew close turned out to be the oak leaf. There, we stopped again. I hoped to see one of the things I had grown to love about our walk: a barely visible pressing of the turf by the people who had gone before us. But we couldn't see the flattened grass where pilgrims of the oak leaf had trod. I guessed that the missing sign and impenetrable plantation had dispersed ramblers on the hill. The sun was setting behind the mountains far to the west and a shadow had moved at walking pace up the field we were standing in, but enough light remained for Hussein to point down the hill to a slight break in a hedge and say, 'there.'

He moved off at an unusually enthusiastic speed, almost breaking into a trot. It was the first time Hussein had led the expedition, and he looked like he was enjoying himself, waving the booklet at a gate in the corner of the next field. We went through that gate into another field where we this time could just make out the path, like a whisper on the grass. What was that Robert Frost phrase? The path in the wood that *wanted wear*. I can't remember if it was the one more or less travelled. This one wanted wear and Hussein and I were happy to supply it, setting off into the gloaming, marking the way for the people who came after us.

Had Robert Frost been talking about walking? Or writing? Who knew? He had made a fine art of talking simultaneously about everything and nothing. But writing and walking have plenty in common. Writing was a hike an author took without leaving their desk.

Completing a chapter gave us a nice buzz, **a writer's high** like completing a walk. On both, you can lose your way, end up lost and be forced to retrace your steps. Doubling back looking for the last way marker in writing was done by holding down the delete button and seeing the words disappear off the screen. A word was a footstep. Forty-four miles, the length of Hussein's and my walk, was 80,000 footsteps, roughly the number of words in a book.

'Hey,' I said, after noticing an arc of pale fungi on the ground, 'magic mushrooms. It's the right time of year and exactly the sort of place they turn up.'

I slowed and stared down at the wet grass. To Hussein I described the characteristic pointed silvery head of the Psilocybin but he wasn't interested either in looking for them, imbibing them or listening to me tell stories of hallucinogenic high jinks, which I thought would enthral and impress a twenty-two-year-old.

'They're a really interesting drug,' I said. 'Totally unprocessed, of course. And organic up here. You get a heightened reality, but don't lose control, and they're not the least bit addictive.'

'Middle class white men and your drugs,' he said. 'Just say no, Guy. That's what you're always telling us.' **Guy had me looking out for magic mushrooms for the rest of the day.**

Out of the gloom of the valley floor a few lights were beginning to glow from windows of farmhouses, barns and cottages. A straight road further away silently pulsed with car lights.

We descended into the outskirts of a community. With the village steeple always in sight, we passed the slack tapes of a pony paddock, a wood store, a deserted holiday home with hooded barbecue, an outlying cottage, then through a gate and onto tarmac, Hussein accelerating as we re-entered familiar life and passed the church with the steeple.

'There's a pub up ahead and I've checked it's still in business. It's 6 p.m.,' I said, 'perfect time for a pint and a packet of crisps.'

We were now marching along the pavement of a quiet road, but up ahead at the cross roads where the Green Dragon was, the traffic was heavier. I imagined some of the drivers would be turning into its car park to get an evening drink and bar meal. We passed a non-conformist chapel and a drive with a No Turning sign. We crossed the road and approached the pub, which had a light on in the window. As I turned the handle I read the sign. CLOSED MONDAYS & TUESDAYS & WEDNESDAY LUNCH.

'For f**** sake,' I said. 'It's closed.'

'When's it open?' Hussein asked.

'The day after tomorrow,' I said.

'I'm hungry, Guy,' said Hussein.

From the Green Dragon we took one of the most depressing cab journeys of my life, back to my car. A tough three hour hike up and down hills was reduced in a car to a five-minute drive. We then drove down the steep lane Hussein had limped on the year before into Welshpool, which felt like a real backward step, found a hotel, and ate a burger, both of us beyond caring what we looked like to the other customers.

Before bed I glanced at the Offa's Dyke Path booklet to see how much more of this hell I had to endure, and while counting the squares on the map, I saw that we were soon passing Bredon Hill. Of A.E.Housman fame. He who wrote *A Shropshire Lad*. He was a young man around the time of the First World War who, instead of fighting, sat on Bredon Hill and wrote soppy poetry. That's what an English Literature degree from Edinburgh University got you. I could remember nothing else about him apart from once, in an act of desperation, mentioning him in an exam that I suspect torpedoed my already badly holed 2:1. There was a poem or a cycle of poems or even a book called *On Bredon Hill*. This was what this walk was all about! At last! A literary connection with the soil we were walking over. A landscape imbued with history, drama and poetry. Oh, England! I thought, trying to find the table with my glass: the greatest land on the globe with the greatest language. I would tell Hussein about it tomorrow. But first I Googled Housman's poetry to put me ahead of the game.

# 11.

I walked out of the inn as I always did after an overnight stay in a British provincial hotel: four pounds heavier, badly hungover and embittered by the bill. It was a sunny morning but the wind had an icy bite.

'Christ, I feel rough,' I said as I limped across the car park. 'Don't worry. I'll be okay after five paracetamols.'

'Why do you do that to yourself?' Hussein asked.

'To fill the yawning hole in my soul,' I said.

'You shouldn't drink so much. It's not good,' Hussein helpfully pointed out.

'But I have to. Ancient ritual demands it, my Muslim friend. There are rules I must adhere to. Like your Ramadan. Upon entering an overnight hostelry, proper white English males of a certain age embark on their own personal festival of alcohol and pork. It's a venerated cultural tradition, the observance of which is mandatory if you wish to follow the footsteps of the elders of the tribe and die from depression, heart attack or sclerosis of the liver, which is the way of our people. Pass me that bottle of water.'

We drove back to the Green Dragon, pulled up in the corner of the car park, placed a note in the window saying we would be back in a couple of days, adjusted our clothing, checked the map carefully and set off in the wrong direction.

After walking for ten minutes along a narrow and grungy verge shying from bullying trucks, searching for the stile marked on the map, I pointed back and we turned round.

I located the stile in the filthy hedge and we dropped down a modern embankment onto the valley floor and set off across a wet field towards the swollen River Severn. The character and mood of the path were new. The hills were above and behind us for once, and we were in flat open country. This was Offa in a different mode. **Offa probably had to walk this part of the path because it's the only flat bit.** There was no sign of his usual habit of finding the most arduous route across the land. But actually, there was no sign of the dyke, nor any old oaks to walk under, nor any remnants of an ancient track under foot. It was possible that the dyke and the path had once taken the line of the dual carriageway that we could occasionally see and always hear to the west, and had been rerouted by a 1970s regional planner to this new position. The path's ruler-straight line diagonally across the field had the feel of a pencil mark drawn across a map, not of a strategic position adopted to keep men and women in loin cloths and woad from launching an attack on fair Albion.

Where a flood had risen and then receded back into the river, it had combed the grass and left traceries of twigs and leaves at high water mark. Foliage borne on the water now festooned gates and fences. Plastic barrels and feed sacks pressed against the hedge, farm waste that hadn't been swept with all the rest into the Severn to be expelled into the Bristol Channel and Atlantic.

I started worrying if I had enough layers on. It seemed existential in intensity. Was my hat too thin? Was I going to be cold all day? Should my vest have been sleeveless? Should I go back to the car and pick up another sweater? These were the walker's anxieties. Also, my left calf hurt. I must have overworked it on the hill yesterday. Was it going to tighten, or pass? I continued to monitor my leg, but when I went back to check whether I was still too cold I found I was sweating under my arms and across my back. Oh no. I had too much on. I was going to have to walk for hours with a coat and jumper in my hand. These inner anxieties were matched by an external bombardment from Hussein who already had me on the run, despite being 50 yards ahead of me.

'I hear Channel 4 are in trouble,' he called, with a hint of triumph.

'I don't watch Channel 4 much,' I said.

'I thought all you liberals did,' he said. 'They did a programme where they built a typical English house in the middle of a tribal village in Africa. African women walking around with their boobies out, you know the sort of thing you lot like to film.' **They got the mother and daughter off of Gogglebox to do the show, I'm guessing to be like a common British family meets an African tribe.**

I let that go.

'They were trying to persuade people,' Hussein went on, 'that the poor in Africa have better lives than the rich West. Like most programmes nowadays. That's what white liberals like to do.' He made it fairly clear with the delivery exactly what he thought of that proposition. But to make sure I had the message he said, 'It's what we call *white people shit.*'

'Who's we?' I asked. 'And what's white people shit when it's at home?'

'We is black people, Guy. Every single day black people see things and think *white people shit.*'

'Like when would you think that?' I asked.

'You never heard it?'

'No.'

Hussein chuckled at the thought. 'You have lived a very sheltered existence,' he said.

'Affirmative,' I said. 'Quite deliberately.' That was not true. I only said it to parry the next dart from the lad. I fancied I lived an adventurous and risky life, not right on the edge, perhaps, but near the edge, safely back a pace or two, close enough to occasionally glance over it and remind myself why I wasn't living actually on it.

'So, what exactly is white people shit?' I asked, trying to make it sound an unimportant subject.

'Camping,' Hussein said. 'Bungee jumping. Sky diving. All white people shit. Don't worry about it, Guy. I could go on for hours.'

'Go on then,' I said.

'White people shit is what white people do when life is too comfortable, to add a bit of excitement. White people also call it a midlife crisis, but you guys go through this at all ages, trekking through a war zone out of choice when there's people actively looking to leave the war zone, or sky diving to experience the thrill of being alive. We black people know we're alive, we are near enough always on high alert in case something happens, so I'd say white people shit is white people doing stupid things to feel alive, a privilege no other race has.'

Hussein had burst a small but significant bubble I had been inhabiting, in which he did not make racial distinctions. Wasn't that what people with black skin were advocating?

'Swimming!' he shouted. 'Swimming with sharks. There's another one. And mountain climbing!'

I caught up with him at another new galvanised kissing gate. A bank of nettles was whitened with clay dust from the flood water.

'All right, what else?' I asked him.

'Running around in the rain for fun. Singing in the rain! What's that about, bro? You people made a film about that. Now that is white people shit. Singing in the rain. What is wrong with you? You don't sing, you shelter in the rain. Having a pet snake, or any pet that shouldn't be a pet. Plus, the biggest one of all,' he replied. 'Walking. In the countryside, for so-called fun. Like we are now. That's white people shit.'

'But it's beautiful, don't you think?' We were on a small rise above the silver river, which flowed past at running speed, carting tree trunks as it went. The bank we stood on wasn't an ancient dyke. Its uniform lines were made with mechanical diggers, probably as a flood defence.

'No,' he said.

'Walking and enjoying the countryside is not white people shit, Hussein. It's cool people shit. Particularly in Britain – a nation of which you are a valued member.'

We walked on in single file for half an hour until I'd got us well positioned under Bredon Hill, and was ready to start my second lecture in Englishness.

'Here,' I waved at the wooded hill, 'we are not just walking through stunning landscape, we are not just walking through history, for a hoard of Roman gold was dug up almost on this spot, but we are also walking

through pages of English poetry. Look over yonder...'
I shouted, to set the tone.

He turned his head and said, 'At that electricity pole?'

'No! Beyond. To Bredon Hill! One of Shropshire's blue remembered hills,' I threw in the Housman line, adding, 'Isn't that a beautiful phrase?'

'Did you write it?' he asked.

'It's good, isn't it?' I said.

'Blue remembered hills is dope, Guy,' said Hussein. 'It's got, like, childhood memories. I'll be honest, it's the first good bit of writing I've ever heard of yours. Fair play.'

'Bredon Hill is the subject of a cycle of poems written in the Victorian era called *A Shropshire Lad*. I didn't write them. Chap called A.E. Housman did. He actually wrote the poem sitting up there.' The last bit I added on to intensify the experience for Hussein. 'Have you heard of him?'

'No.'

'Great lyric poetry.' I said, and threw out my hand theatrically.

*Into my heart an air that kills*
*From yon far country blows:*
*What are those blue remembered hills*
*What spires, what farms are those?*

*That is the land of lost content*
*I see it shining plain*
*The happy highways where I went*
*And cannot come again.*

I was beginning to tear up. I felt magnificent. This was what our walk was all about: Hussein's induction into the sacred state of being British, via the agency of English poetry in the Shropshire hills.

'And Elgar,' I continued. I took a stab at his Christian name, but thought I was probably safe from being corrected by Hussein, 'Arthur Elgar,[1] the great British composer, lived not far south of here. In the sublime Wye Valley. We could do that on our next walk.'

Hussein gave me a look of derision, so I moved on.

'Have you heard of *The Enigma Variations*?'

Hussein looked blank.

I started humming the opening bars (as I saw them) of Nimrod. 'Hold on,' I said. 'Let's Spotify it.'[2] In a minute we were listening. As the music swelled and met the rolling of the timpani and the blasting horns, my eyes teared up again with emotion. 'Isn't this the best music you've ever heard?' I shouted.

He put his head to one side.

I hummed along, tears now streaming down my cheeks. 'It's basically the musical equivalent of being British,' I explained. 'It stirs the heart, and reminds us that we – that includes you my friend! – the English, the British, are the greatest nation on the face of globe. Come here and let me put my arm around you as we listen to it again together,' I said.

'No,' said Hussein.

'All right, don't be touchy,' I said, turning it down. 'Look, I'm not saying wherever you came from, in Africa, wasn't without any music or poetry,' Hussein narrowed his eyes, 'but Britain,' I continued, 'hopefully

---

[1] It's Edward.
[2] I recommend you do the same as you read these next pages.

you're beginning to see this yourself. Britain is more richly steeped in history and literature than anywhere else, basically. Can you feel it at all?'

'Let me see,' Hussein leant back his head and closed his eyes. I smiled – the lad was finally getting it. He looked back at me and opened his eyes. 'Er. No,' he said. 'Nothing. Sorry, Guy. Oh no, hold on. I feel something. In my right foot. It's wet. Is that what you mean?'

I tutted. 'Okay. Listen to this,' I countered, getting out my phone and scrolling. 'Housman again,' I said, picking a random poem thinking they'd all be sentimental-young-man-comes-to-terms-with-his-sexuality-in-an-era-of-prohibition. 'Same year as the music.'

*To skies that knit their heartstrings right*
*To fields that bred them brave*
*The saviours come not home tonight*
*Themselves they could not save*

Hussein said, 'Shall we keep going?'

'No!' I shouted. 'This is about the sacrifices the young men of this parish made for us. For you and me, Hussein. To build our nation. Listen:

*In dawns in Asia, tombstones show*
*And Shropshire names are read*
*And the Nile spills his overthrow*
*Beside the Severn's dead.*

I pointed to the river.

*We pledge in peace by farms and town*
*The queen they served in war,*

'That's Queen Victoria by the way,

*And fire the beacons up and down*
*The land they perished for.*
*God save the queen! we living sing*
*From height to height 'tis heard*
*And with the rest your voices ring;*
*Lads of the fifty-third.'*

'Isn't that stirring?' I ask.

'Are you aware of what they were doing? By the banks of the Nile?' Hussein asked.

'Of course I am, look, I'm not saying the British Empire was perfect, I'm just saying it was noble and very often beautiful. And the poet asks us to consider their sacrifice. Doesn't that mean anything to you? All those young lives lost?'

'They were pillaging Africa, Guy. They were stealing our resources.' **They still are.**

'But you're British. You are on the other side now, Hussein. Be proud of it. This is British history I'm teaching you. You are British. Forget that African stuff.'

'Jesus, Guy.' He said.

'You ended up on the winning side,' I said. 'Congratulations.'

He walked off, and I caught him up on the path along the top of the grassy bund.

'Hey,' I said, 'I was just having a tease. You will discover, if you read more, he's actually a pretty good lyric poet.'

'Lyric as in dance hall?' Hussein asked.

'Yes. That's where the term comes from. Lyric poetry is personal and sensitive, about emotions and feelings. Poetry, well, all writing, started being about God, then about kings and queens, and finally became about ourselves. Housman was gay. It was totally unacceptable then.'

'You think he invented rapping?'

'Not exactly, but he was an early exponent of using a metre and rhyme to express his feelings. He was talking about his own experience. It had never been done before. Lyric poetry.'

'White people invented that, did they?'

'Yes. I mean the poets from that period were, I believe, all white, because of the social and political system in place at the end of the eighteenth-century.'

'You think white people invented rap lyrics?'

'I have tried to explain—' I said.

'—Is that why there are so many white rappers?' he asked.

We plodded across water meadow after water meadow, from time to time meeting the swollen river scurrying past us. I stood and stared at the muscle-bound water but Hussein didn't glance in its direction. He was dragging his feet, going slower and slower, which was a problem because we still had nearly twenty miles ahead of us to cover. Every time I stopped and looked back, he was further away. He was playing a game of reverse grandmother's footsteps.

'What's up?' I asked.

'I've sprained my side,' he said, holding his right-hand side.

'You mean you've got a stitch?'

'No. I sprained it.'

'How could you? You haven't lifted anything.'

116

There were aspects of Hussein's understanding of anatomy and medicine that were confounding. 'It's because I got too cold,' he said. **My people were made for the temperatures in Africa, centuries of adapting to thrive in Africa, so obviously my muscles and bones probably have an optimum temperature higher than Guy's.**

'Walk faster,' I said.

'No, I need Mumma's oil.'

Mumma's oil was often referred to. It was from Kenya and could ease all muscular and joint pain, and, interestingly, stop you feeling cold. I told him that was bullshit, but Hussein swore by it. **I've got a cousin who makes a herbal oil, and that stuff works.** He insisted that the reason he felt cold was not because there was an icy north wind that cut through his inadequate clothing but because he hadn't had a rub of Mumma's oil.

I decided to walk on and let him catch up. We had been in open country all morning, but now the path brushed close to a hamlet, and took a narrow way between the river and a larch-lap fence, in the gloom under some overgrown leylandii. There was one of those pub tables on the river bank where it looked as though the occupants of the house on the other side of the fence sat in the summer. I caught a whiff of a stealthy attempt to privatise a public space. The house was empty; you could sense the cold dark rooms behind the thin curtains. The barbeque was rusting by the patio doors. It was like all holiday homes, not fully loved.

I sat at the table and unlaced my boots. With a sharp sting I withdrew my foot, peeled back the sock and looked at the raw circle deep in the skin on my heel. I was carrying in my rucksack a spare pair of thin socks. It was unusual to have something useful on board. I stared at my bare feet. The air was cold, the ground muddy, and my skin was a pale yellow. I wanted Hussein to see my blister to show him the sacrifice I was prepared to make for our walk, so I waited, staring at the willow leaves on the grass.

Hussein approached at the speed of a bored shopper trailing behind his wife in a department store. He sat down heavily, as though at the end of a very long walk, which was not good as we were barely a third of the way through a very long walk. We still had six hours to go that day, let alone the next day and the one after.

'Teresa May's not having a very easy time, wouldn't you say?' Hussein said. 'That ERG group with Rees-Mogg are blocking her.'

'Yes,' I said. Along the way, I had somehow been cast as defender of Brexit. 'So it seems.'

'You know what I heard?' Hussein said. 'I heard that in Europe, Great Britain is a laughing stock.'

'I doubt very much they are really laughing at Great Britain, Hussein. The clue is in the name – Great. I'm sure they're jealous of us getting away and being free from the dead hand of the Commission. They just won't admit it.'

As I forced my foot back into the stiff boot, miming heroic bravery, I wondered why I was doing this walk, as it hadn't turned out to be much fun, or indeed, considering the contempt Hussein now held Britain in, much use.

Hussein said, 'Looks like that rain cloud is coming this way. Have you seen it? It is dark, man. That usually means heavy rain, I believe.'

My foot was agony to force down in the boot, but once I had tightened the laces and stood up, the pain got worse.

'Come on, we better get going,' I said.

I left Hussein emptying the contents of his rucksack on the table looking for something, and limped off down the path, wondering how much more torture was in store for me that afternoon.

Going by his miserable gait, it looked like Hussein was also wondering why we were doing this. How happy he had looked before we started our project, sitting on a sofa in Tottenham, scrolling through his phone while toddlers crawled over him, staring at the stewards loading the starters for the 2.15 at Haydock Park. The council flat may have been hot, crowded and noisy, but it was Hussein's comfort zone. Unlike the Offa's Dyke footpath on a blowy autumn day in the Welsh borders.

I stopped for a rest at a stile and, looking back, saw that that the pub table was still visible. I estimated that we were now resting longer than walking. In fact, Hussein had taken a rest between the pub table and the stile. I watched him inching his way towards me, now travelling at the speed of someone looking for a valuable ring they had dropped.

The path took us down a leafy farm track and then up a flight of steps to a trunk road. After waiting for a gap between the thundering lorries, we crossed over, and then held a long and not entirely enjoyable map scrutiny session. It seemed we were to walk for 3 miles along the verge.

I could see that the path had definitely been rerouted at the same time as the bypass was built, probably in the 70s. I could easily imagine a bloke with a slide rule in Cardiff. He's chatting to his boss. 'I've pulled out those troublesome oaks, and routed the old Offa's Dyke footpath along the new road. No one walks anyway.'

This wasn't Offa's style at all: tarmac, traffic noise and strewn litter. And there was a lot of litter. Fag packs, lighters, beer bottles, wine bottles, cans, single trainers, rope, car trim, children's clothes, disposable nappies, all of which I assumed had been chucked out of vehicles. If I had my way a crack team of forensic scientists would DNA test every single item down to the cellophane on a pack of cigarettes, and then track down each and every culprit, charge, try and sentence them to a minimum ten-year tariff. Or would I put them in chain gangs to clear up all the A roads in Britain? I smiled at the thought. I hadn't smiled for miles. And they would not be issued with those pincer things that save you bending down to pick stuff up. Or gloves. And they would be stood over by a guy with a shotgun and dark glasses, to keep them honest.

'You know what the national minimum wage is in some states in America?' Hussein shouted between trucks.

Here we go, I thought. I was fairly confident it would not be a high figure. It wasn't Hussein's style to point out the finer aspects of life in the capitalist West.

'Twelve dollars?' I said.

'No Guy,' he said, happily. 'You are way off. It's two dollars twenty-five an hour in Alabama for waiters.' I **think the two dollar minimum wage for waiters is the norm in most American states.**

'I find that hard to believe,' I said. Somehow, I had got into the position of defending the Alabama state legislature.

'They are expected to make it up with tips.'

'Surely not,' I said.

'Yeah,' said Hussein, barely hiding his triumph. He then said 'Do you tip, Guy?'

'Not five hundred per cent!' I said.

'Well,' he said, laying the blame for poverty in the Deep South fairly and squarely at my door.

We continued to trudge down the verge, looking like a couple of hobos, until we were taken by the sign of the oak leaf over a stile and onto a wonderfully quiet canal path, beside a deserted canal sprinkled with pondweed and willow leaves. It was a blessing to be on the level firm ground of the towpath. Hussein, flushed with the joy of surprising me about how poorly paid American hospitality staff were, started singing *Old Man River*. Now he was really hamming it up. Next thing he'd be handing me a whip.

# 12.

The Montgomeryshire Canal was a strip of water built along the side of the hills between Llanymynech and Welshpool, a distance of 34 miles. The bit Hussein and I found ourselves walking along looked exactly as it would have when completed in 1821. The shallow canal, the tow path wide enough for a shire horse, the humpback bridges, each with its cast iron number on an enamelled oval plate, the hand operated drawbridge, the lock gates and the lock keeper's cottage, all these things were pleasingly untouched by the passing years. I stared at the water locks and admired their simplicity.

'Out of earshot of the road, and with no one around we are in an entirely eighteenth-century landscape. Incredible, eh?' I said to Hussein.

He glanced at me and held his stare, saying nothing. He seemed angry. He didn't look at the lock gates, I didn't know why. Hussein had an implacable mode, and he was deep in it right now.

'These lock gates are a product of an analogue world, now lost,' I said.

He didn't seem interested and turned to move off, albeit slowly. It was one of the joys of our walk that the path had a habit of taking us back in time: we had been through the crusades, high Victoriana, 1970s regional development, and were now pulled back to early industrialisation, the moment in the history of the world when, depending on your viewpoint, everything either started to go right or wrong.

'It's a historic landscape, Hussein,' I called to his back. 'The canals could move large cargoes of iron and coal for the first time. They were the foundation of the Industrial Revolution. Are you aware the industrialisation of the entire globe kicked off thirty miles from here? This canal would have been at the leading edge of global technology when it was built.'

'The Industrial Revolution,' Hussein said.

'That's the one!' I said, proudly. 'One of our many gifts to an ungrateful world.'

'It's what you did after killing Africans for money, wasn't it?'

I ignored that.

'The engineering that was pioneered here,' I said, 'was sent out all over the world. We built harbours, bridges...'

'And the trains in India and Africa,' Hussein said. 'Don't forget them.'

'They are a very good case in point. Thank you. They are still in working order today. A magnificent transportation system designed and built by the British.'

'The British did not build them, Guy. Forced foreign labour did.'

'Well, we told them what to do. Gave them tools.'

'What? Pickaxes?'

'Organised them...' I felt on slightly marshy ground, possibly leading to quicksand, so stopped talking.

'It's a thing you white people often do, say how good the railways are in countries you colonised. You

124

know what the railways were for? Not for transporting Africans or Indians around. They were made to freight out all the things you stole from us more easily. That and moving troops around to kill us. And now you want us to admire them! It's like a gang comes round to your house, right, rapes your wife and daughter, steals the TV and I say to you, yeah, but did you see how cool their getaway car was? We're not interested in the trains, ok? We're interested in the crimes.[1] Anyway, we got the Chinese to build much better railways now if we want.'

'I wouldn't get involved with them if I were you,' I said.

'After our experience with the Europeans we're not holding our breath for anything much. At least the Chinese don't murder us, torture us, make us convert to their religion, eat their food and learn their language.'

---

[1]Hussein here, sliding into Guy's footnotes. I don't think anyone's actually attempted to quantify how much was/is taken from Africa. And I don't think the monetary value is the most important part, though it is massive. The biggest cost of what was/is being done is culturally, spiritually and environmentally. The first two I believe were done intentionally, the third I think is just a case of they didn't/don't care. The British Museum stole our history and denied lots of it. Ethiopia was a country and Africa a continent which puts a huge emphasis on spirituality, unlike you lot. But you went out of your way to remove our spiritual artefacts, like the Emperor's hair in Westminster Abbey, to subjugate and abuse us. Least important is the gold, silver, ivory, diamonds, rubies, coal, not forgetting oil with all those dodgy contracts, and all the other commodities you robbed. De Beers is worth 6 billion pounds today, and we all know where they started. Billions? Trillions, if it was all added together.

'They'll nick all your minerals.'

'That's the going rate for a road these days.'

We walked on in silence, then I said, 'But there were positive things we did in the UK.'

'What?'

'The power loom,' I said, 'the steam engine, iron casting, the first precision tools. Phenomenal advances. All British. Up until then people had been pulling sacks of turnips around on carts with square wheels and knocking together two legged tables with bits of wood. We, Britain, that's your country, Hussein, gave them manufacturing and mass production. Isn't that something to be proud of?'

'We were taught it at school,' he said. 'It's when you went from exploiting foreigners to exploiting your own people. A real step forward.'

I was taught about the Industrial Revolution at school, too, in the 70s, under the flickering lights of the three-day week, during strikes we were annoyed our teachers did not participate in. The early nineteenth century was depicted as a time when British engineering, design, manufacturing and entrepreneurship were world beating, and the nation could actually achieve something, in sharp contrast to the slackerdom of the 1970s.

Later, when I Googled the history of the Monty, as this canal was known, it turned out that its construction was a sequence of balls-ups, worthy of the 1970s. One of the arches of the aqueduct collapsed under dubious circumstances and the chief engineer absconded to America. It is not recorded what he built there. Breaches were common, leaving the few barges that used it stuck in mud on the bottom of an empty canal for weeks while the hole was located and plugged. But the main problem was that nobody really wanted to carry goods from Llanymynech to Welshpool. The route didn't take off like Manchester to Liverpool. The income from the tolls was disappointing and the business barely viable. A lifeline was thrown in the form of the railways, which were laying tracks across Britain and often bought out the canals to build on them. It made sense: both needed to be straight and flat. Our man in charge of the Monty declared the railways a passing fad, and he rejected the generous offer the men with the rails put on the table. The Monty went bankrupt. **Knowing the Brits' natural skill of failing upwards he probably ended up becoming a politician in charge of canals and waterways in the rest of the Empire.**

The canal silted up and was cut off from the main network, leaving the Monty a 30 mile stretch of water that went from nowhere to nowhere. All the little communities north of Welshpool which had hoped to be the new Sheffields and Manchesters remained rural backwaters, untouched by the industrialisation that propelled towns like Birmingham and Wolverhampton, aka The Workshop of the World, to glorious riches and international stardom. Welshpool and Llanymynech became The Garden Shed of the World. Even the Monty's modern fate was bad. In the 70s a plan was put together to restore the missing section so that it could link to the main grid and attract a few tourist cruises, but this was opposed by the local council. I had to read that twice, but the council didn't want the responsibility of dealing with the infill so The Monty was left isolated and unused.

Pondweed and lilies dotted the water. Hussein had stopped again and stared into the water. He was clearly undelighted by the lock gates and the engineering. I too looked into the reflection on the canal. The water was surprisingly shallow. I didn't want Hussein to be pissed off. But he did look miserable. I had shown him this beautiful canal and in two leaps we were talking about African genocide.

'Are you okay?' I said.

'You say you want to go on this walk together and talk about things, but you never listen to what I say,' Hussein said. 'You make jokes. That's what you think of what I say.'

I thought, *these youngsters are so soft*, and said, 'I'm sorry Hussein, I don't want you to be unhappy. I'll be careful what I say.'

The path left the canal at the lock keeper's cottage, a building as futile for a canal with no boats on it as everything else suddenly felt.

I watched Hussein limping behind me, his right hand holding his side. We emerged from the leafy tunnel into muted sunshine on open fields. Here amongst the tall reeds and squelchy grass, the Monty petered out. How often the promoter must have stood on this spot and cursed that his canal didn't reach the main network and riches.

Hussein didn't appreciate the poignancy of the spot and brushed past me. When I started catching up with him, he accelerated, despite the limp, which I now believed to be optional. I didn't persist; my blister was stinging. I decided to try and divert his attention from the woes of the walk, and picked a remark to shout at him that would appeal to his anti-Western bent.

'It must have been a beautiful world before airplanes, cars and railways, before the internal combustion engine, before steam. A simpler world. **A world where it takes several days to walk a distance you could cover in less than an hour today, I feel their pain.** Everything being drawn at walking pace by a shire horse.' I was moving into over-compensation territory here, a wide and open place I often found myself caught in, with no way out, when talking to black and brown people. There, I said things like, 'Oh I've been to Africa, I loved the Ngorongoro Crater.' Or, 'you're from Antigua? It's such a beautiful island. What an amazing place to grow up. I stayed at the Calabash Gardens Hotel. I love the beach there.'

I ploughed on with Hussein: 'It would be so much better if vegetables weren't flown in cargo holds around the world. The way they are now. At the supermarket, I can buy fresh beans from Asia, and apples from South Africa, in mid-winter. We should eat seasonally. You can get strawberries all year round nowadays. It's wrong. We need to go back to a simpler way of life.'

He drew to a halt at the gate and gave me a withering look.

'It ain't gonna happen, Guy,' he said. 'People are going to want strawberries all year round and other people are gonna sell them.'

Aggrieved. That's what Hussein was. He gazed off towards a wood. I noticed his expression. It was the prince in exile. His face seemed to burn with injustice.

'Come on,' I said, moving off.

'No. I got to rest a bit,' Hussein said.

It was beginning to feel like a bad first date. One in which neither of us turned out to look as good as our profile picture. I don't know if his bleak mood was because he was in pain, or he was pissed off with me for either starting this stupid walk, or being white, or for invading Abyssinia in 1868. **All of them. Plus I was in pain.**

One of us had to make a move. It certainly wasn't going to be Hussein, and the truth was that for some time now my jokes had felt lamer and his arguments sturdier.

'Hussein, listen to me a moment,' I said, turning to face the spindly-legged figure. 'Look. I admit it. We fucked up,' I said.

'We haven't lost our way again, have we?'

'No. I'm talking about something else. I'm saying we, the English, the British, white people, we came over to Africa and we ... we could have behaved a lot better.'[2]

'What?' Hussein said, screwing the top on his aluminium water bottle and putting it his knapsack.

'We went to Africa and we did bad things. You are right. We didn't do the right thing. I'm sorry. I see it, I admit it and I am sorry.'

'Why are you apologising to me?'

'Because I want to show you that I sympathise with you. Colonialism was the act of a bully. But I also hoped you see that a lot of good things came from it too. I mean, not just bad.'

He chose to ignore that.

'We went over there. We misbehaved. We, the British, actually fucked up. I see what you are saying, and how you feel. But we've woken up. And now it's time to do the right thing. Because we can't wallow in shame. That's no way to live. Acknowledge what's gone wrong,

[2]As I said this I KNEW it wasn't enough.

say *yes, we did it,* and get on and do better. Build trust. Slowly. Do the next best thing. The correct thing. Act like humans, or as close to humans as the English can get. Can you not forgive us?'

'What?' he said. 'No, no, no I can't,' he took a bite of his apple. I noticed his apples were better than mine, again. 'Anyway, what does it matter what I think? It's nothing to do with me. And what help is forgiveness? It doesn't do anything. No. No.'

He stayed still, sort of quivering with anger or frustration, so I walked past him. I realised I was blushing.

He held his apple and looked at it. 'Hold on,' he said. 'Imagine, Guy, what would have happened if you had come to Africa and dealt with us straight. Had not stolen things, but traded with us in an honest way. Respected us.'

'Goods from the West Indies during slavery would probably have not got the Fairtrade sticker at the Co-op,' I said.

'You never know,' said Hussein. 'These schemes are often white man scams, you know?'

'It's an interesting thought, though,' I said. 'If Britain had traded fairly and squarely with Africa, rather than stolen what we wanted, you would be rich. Africa would be powerful.'

'Why would you have traded fairly with Africa? You are into stealing and thieving, bro.'

We came off the fields and found ourselves limping down an avenue of ancient oaks each the girth of a car. Their roots were anacondas on the dry earth. I looked up to see ten thousand oak leaves and no sky. These hardwoods were no more than 300 years old but I felt

131

they stood in the place of trees that had stood as long in the same avenue, going back to Offa himself. I could easily see Offa decreeing the scheme.

'Plant these oak saplings in two lines, and make sure they are each thirty paces apart. That one's too close. Dig it up and move it. I'm taking the men up that hill there. Yes. The steep one. Yes. That's where we're going.'

I was admiring a docile herd of black and white Friesians lying by a concrete water trough when Hussein said, 'I don't like cows, Guy.'

He was an urban lad. When he saw a flock of Welsh mountain sheep above Welshpool he had said, 'Look, white cattle.'

'They're fine,' I said. 'They won't bother us. I'm not frightened of them.'

'If they come at us, I'll push you towards them and run.'

He walked away laughing.

Over another little lane we entered a reedy field with cloven hoof prints in the long grass, and I accepted the growing feeling I had that we were actually now on two walks. His and mine.

I grumbled to myself about this. I was like, *can't you let it go, for a moment, Hussein? You should have more gratitude for the UK*. But I didn't really fancy saying either of those things to him.

I trudged on. My boots felt too heavy, like there was something wrong.

I looked at their bottoms. I don't know what I was expecting to find. A clod of guilt?

# 13.

We crossed another tarmacked strip of the twenty-first century as lorries thundered past us on the main road, and then hobbled out across the timeless fields. Hussein was lagging again. I waited by a new galvanised kissing gate, and looked up on Google why it was so named. I had always thought it was because it had a tendency to make people press up against each other, and I guess to share a quick kiss, but it was actually because the gate only kissed the posts, rather than latching onto them.

I said to Hussein, when he caught up and stopped for a rest, 'I have a theory that we might never have learnt to combine trade with murder were it not for the transatlantic slave trade. You see that's what's at the root of all of this. It was that greedy, vicious business plan to enslave people for profit that's at the bottom of British racism. It's money. Before slavery in the Americas, black people were accorded respect in Britain.'

'How do you know?'

'Have you ever read *Othello*?'

'No,' said Hussein.

'It's a play by Shakespeare, also not written far from here, and fascinating for many reasons,' (Hussein threw his eyes skywards) 'but its main interest to us, on this walk, is that it is a play about a black man. Yet it's not about racism. Quite the reverse, people in the play worship Othello. How can that be? Shakespeare knew all there was to know about the world around him. He had the secret of every human heart, and the words to express them. He wrote about guilt, shame, ambition, cowardice, love, lust everything ... but he never wrote about racism. He put a black man in a play but even then it wasn't about racism. It was about jealousy. How could that be?'

Hussein put up his hand as though in class. 'Yes?' I said, brightening at the thought Hussein was engaging.

'How long are you going to be? Only I'm getting cold again.'

'Let's walk then.'

We crossed a deserted muddy lane and were faced with the sheer cliff of a disused quarry. I looked at the map. The two most disappointing words on an OS map are HILL FORT. We had seen at least five marked, all of which turned out, when we eagerly approached them, to be nothing more than a bump in the ground when we had been hoping for battlements and moats and even helmets and swords sticking out of the ground.

'The reason Shakespeare didn't write a play about racism was because he didn't see it. Why? Because Othello was written, and Shakespeare lived, before the transatlantic slave trade. Think of the play that Shakespeare would have written about racism. But he never knew it. He died in 1616. Only 3% of the Africans who were transported to the Americas had been taken from Africa when Shakespeare died.'

'Oh, right,' said Hussein with little interest or enthusiasm.

'Slavery was first and foremost a totally crap business scheme, that then relied on extreme racism to work.[1] As the money rolled in from the sugar and tobacco plantations across the Atlantic, people in the UK must have asked how such things were possible. Doubts they expressed that enslaving people was wrong had to be quashed at every turn, to keep the money flowing. Slavery caused racism. Greed and amorality caused slavery. And slavery turned all the British into racists when they saw how rich they were getting. *Let's not ask too many questions here, eh?* Like the banking crisis, or Bophal or any of the hundreds of money-making themes developed by the British which dispensed with human dignity and rights.'

I never thought Hussein took much of an interest in the fate of the slaves. He was angrier about British colonial activities. His ancestors were in Ethiopia, thousands of miles of inhospitable desert away from the crimes. Plus, there was the small detail of his family being in the trade (in a good way).

We pressed on up a steep muddy track and were met by a couple, the woman of which wore tight white trousers and white trainers which she was trying to keep clean. Short distance walkers. We had passed their car parked on the lane.

'Amateurs,' I said.

I was panting for breath on the hill but I wanted to get Hussein's attention. 'Imagine if the prick who said *let's*

---

[1] The first slaves taken to the Americas were white Irish. When they perished of tropical diseases, some evil creep came up with the idea of forcibly transporting people from the tropics of Africa.

*get the Africans to work for nothing* had been told to shut up. And the notion of slavery being utterly wrong was settled in 1600 and not 1830. How different the world would be.'

'You would be a lot poorer,' Hussein said. 'You, personally, and the whole of Britain. England would be like a budget Poland,' he smiled.

'And how rich would Africa be?' I asked, and allowed him time to think about that.

'We would have all the gold, all the diamonds, the oil, the copper, uranium... and we would have traded them with you for a proper price. We would have been decent, bro.' he cried out. 'And traded, not thieved.'

'We would now be talking Arabic, or an African language,' I said. 'English is out of the picture as an international language.'

'You would have had to learn Arabic,' Hussein said.

Towards the top of the quarry, some well-meaning people had built a concrete and metal map to illustrate some landmarks in the landscape that stretched out for many miles. We stopped and leant on it, looking out over a wide, sunlit valley floor, with its silver river weaving across it.

'And black people would be a rarity in Britain, I guess,' I said, 'without slavery or colonisation.'

Hussein had turned his face away from me. He wasn't taking in the view. At least he didn't look like it.

'Think of the kind of place Britain might have been if it had not made the calamitous, the deadly decision to enter the slave trade,' I repeated. 'It would be a Britain that saw Africans as cool foreigners from hot, distant lands, who had a different, often better, way of doing things. And the African way, which you are so fond of, would be accepted on an equal footing with the European.'

I saw an example of exactly the opposite values, plodding up the hill towards us. A group was heading in our direction. You could tell they were a group because the leaders were two women in their late twenties dressed in outdoor clothes and exuding positivity and fitness. Between them was a girl with hair over her face and a miserable woman dressed in the kind of track suit which you wouldn't see on a running track. The group leaders had lanyards and ID cards. There was a whiff of care home or even parole about them. The lead woman looked at me and I knew what was about to happen. Yes. She gave me a look that said, 'Same gig, eh?' I knew that nothing I could do would remove from her mind the idea that I was in some way in charge of Hussein. I hoped Hussein hadn't noticed.

He had noticed something different. When their group had passed well out of earshot he said, 'Offa's dykes.'

'They'd be offended at that,' I said, 'without even noticing themselves how they had casually categorised us. What a frigging world.'

'I think being black makes it okay to make tasteless remarks about other minorities,' Hussein said. I clapped him on the back and laughed.

'It's a sodding mess,' I said.

Hussein remained looking out at the valley. Something made me say, 'Do you remember coming to England as a child?'

He nodded. He didn't smile. 'You mean leaving Africa?' His chin was high. 'I was excited,' he said flatly. 'I was excited but it was cold, and depressingly grey.'

'Do you know where you arrived?'

'Gatwick. Then we went to stay in a friend's flat in Acton. I had my first ever packet of cheese and onion crisps as we waited for the bus, which I thought were absolute filth – the crisps, not the bus. I thought the bus was cool as fuck and sat in the middle seats by the window looking out, slightly scared, thinking, *This is it. This is my new life. Scary.* But I was also happy for the exact same reason: *this is my new life.*'

He remained staring into the distance. He had had a happy childhood in the hidden courtyards of the houses on the east coast of Africa, playing on the flat roofs under the stars, running through the shady alleys to the beach. I could see how swapping that with Gatwick on a rainy February morning could hurt. I had often seen huddled Muslim families standing on the pavement at the airport when I was sweeping through on a foreign vacation. I could have passed a nine-year-old Hussein and his mum and the kids waiting anxiously for their cousins' minibus.

'I had arrived in the country I had seen in the movies and on the BBC news. I love the cheese and onion Walkers now, and still love sitting on the window seats on the bus, looking out watching the houses.' He tutted and walked on.

At our next break, with a gnarled old wood below us and the promise of a heath above, we stopped again.

'Do you know why we're doing this?' I asked.

'What?'

'Walking the Offa's Dyke Path together.'

'Mental health, innit?' Hussein said, and then laughed bitterly, shaking his head. 'I think mine's got worse.'

'Today's not been easy,' I said.

'Why are we doing it, Guy?' he peeled off his rucksack. 'It's a good question.'

I was thinking, how would it feel if I said *Let's scrap this walk eh, Hussein? What do you say we call a taxi back to the car? We could be in London by this evening.* But a rather annoying voice, one I had often tried to silence in other contexts, said *You can't quit, Guy.*

'We can't quit, Hussein,' I said. 'I know you're unhappy and your back hurts.'

'It's my side muscle, I sprained it,' he said.

'And my foot is agony. And we've got twenty tough miles to go. I admit the situation is dire. But we can't give up. Do you know why?'

Hussein looked dismayed. 'It's not because we're British is it?'

'Er, no.' I said. 'Not in this case.'

'Well what is it?' He asked.

'It's because we have said we would complete the journey. And because too much rests on us doing exactly that.'

'Oh,' said Hussein, 'it's not your book is it?'

'No! It's much more important than that.'

'What is?'

'This is about our friendship, the relationship between black and white, old and young, Muslim and Christian. We are a walking unit of racial and religious collaboration, integration and, dare I say it, my friend: love. We can't quit that project. We have been thrown together in one family, by the arrival of two children, Shoaib and May. You and I are a working model of racial and generational integration. If we can't make this work ... well, there's no alternative. We have to. The immigrants aren't leaving this country, and nor are the white people. We have to walk together.'

Hussein stood up, shouldered his ruck sack, and without looking at me said, 'We better get on, then.'

Thinking about that took up about a mile. I hardly noticed my surroundings or the path. It was green and there were some gates and stiles. We were on a mission. I smiled. And there was soon more good news. At a broken gate I looked on the map and saw, only a page and half further along the path, an icon of a blue beer mug.

'There's a place to stop quite close,' I said.

# 14.

The path went along the side of a steep hill, and we slowly ascended onto a bit of heathland which felt ancient, uninhabited and unowned, except by the sky. The oak leaf led us between scrubby bushes of hawthorn and holly and tussocks of long dry grasses. To our left the land fell away into a valley and rose again miles away as deep dark hills under the brooding sky.

We tramped across the plateau and as we started descending Hussein said, 'Look.'

There it was, a long mound of uneven earth about forty feet high and thirty feet wide. It reared up on our left, a disturbing shape because it was so big and obviously man made, but not contoured by digger or any mechanical machine. There was something indisputably pre-wheelbarrow about its crude, rough, rude finish. The Dyke. It spoke of leather and tallow and wool and wood. It was made in 788 but it looked like it had been finished six months ago. It was built by a Dane, miles from his home, to mark the edge of his empire. When we Googled this section we learnt that there was actually a second mound built in parallel, called Wat's Dyke. The arrangement was that the Celts were not allowed over Offa's Dyke and the Saxons weren't allowed over Wat's

Dyke, so people could meet and trade and flirt or do all of the things they wanted on the strip of land in the middle.

It was the first time we had seen such an apparently undisturbed length of the dyke. I imagined men in skins and leather piling mud on mud, sliding around on the greasy clay. It must have been filthy work. Then I imagined a bunch of Celts in furs appear over its top brandishing swords and banging them on shields. Hussein and I would be well back from the back line, lobbing rotting sheep at them with a trebuchet. Hussein would have built the trebuchet for Offa. Hussein would have been famous in Offa's army. The black Muslim with the tricks of war in the sleeves of his robes. North African technology. Islamic maths. *Someone go and get the pasha to aim it.* He had given them the edge in set pieces and sieges. He was a lucky mascot, a talisman in every battle. That was how it should have been.

Hussein, with his fastidious ablutions and pristine white gowns, was always clean and perfumed even on campaign. I was the mud and blood splattered captain begging Hussein to leave his scalloped pavilion to aim the trebuchet. The Saxons were thugs. That huge mud slug we were looking at was basically their equivalent of the Great Wall of China. How grimy and rough the first millennium must have been in the borders.

We trudged on towards the blue beer mug. Neither of us was in a good place. For a start, we were three miles south of a pint of beer. We took on another draining climb onto another heath looking only for the way marker posts. We didn't really care about anything else. We were at the end of our tethers.

142

We limped into the village of Four Crosses as though off a battlefield after a defeat. We ignored the war memorial and shuffled up to the pub. As I got closer, I saw the signs that it might be closed, and dismissed them. 1. Empty car park. *The locals came on foot.* 2. The front door was shut. *The door was round the side.* 3. A sign which, from a distance, looked like it said CLOSED. *They never turned it.* 4. The door was locked. *The one at the side would be open.* I went round the side. There wasn't a door round the side.

I sat on the step and got out my phone saying, 'I need a drink and I am not walking another yard. I'm calling a taxi.'

My mobile ran out of juice as I turned it on. Hussein didn't have one. I couldn't walk anymore, and had taken off my boots because the blister stung so sharply. I couldn't get my foot back in, even if I wanted to. It felt the size of a football.

Eventually, I stood up, picked up my boots and limped in my socks down the high street with Hussein behind me, looking for a café or pub, but there was nothing until we came across an independent garage. The lady behind the counter watched me as I walked in holding my boots, and stayed staring when she saw Hussein behind. What were we to her? Hobos. Prisoners escaping jail? A man who couldn't afford boots that fit? To compensate for and try to divert from the wet footprints I was leaving with my dirty socks I took plenty of confectionery to the counter.

'Buy anything you want, we're not homeless and poor,' I didn't shout to Hussein, but wanted to.

I paid with my card and said, 'I don't suppose there's any way you could call a taxi for us, only my phone has run out of battery and my son-in-law and I are on a long walk for charity and we need to get back to our car?'

As we went outside to wait for our taxi Hussein said quietly, 'for charity.'

We spent the night at a friend's house in the borders, miserable and crippled. We seemed to have tested to destruction the proposition that walking improved physical and mental health. Over dinner we started calling off the walk again, and confirmed it the morning when we could barely hobble down for breakfast, though I bravely managed it when I smelt the bacon.

I drove Hussein back to Tottenham, even though we had established he didn't self-immolate on a train. His princely sense of entitlement irked that day. In retaliation, after I dropped him off at the stained buildings and splattered streets of Tottenham, I bought and ate a pork pie.

We only had covered 20 miles of the walk, and had 22 to go to our destination.

# 15.

We didn't walk again in 2019. Hussein kept making excuses. Then he went to Africa, with assorted family and friends. He told me they took twenty-three huge suitcases, filled with clothes for their relatives. They stayed for six weeks in Mombasa, Kenya, with cousins, where the kids were sent to a Madrassa 'to improve their discipline', Hussein informed me.

On his return I suggested we do some more walking, but Hussein was moving house. The journey which had started for Hussein's mum in Somalia and had included Mombasa and Tottenham now took an unlikely new direction to Denbigh, in North Wales, over 200 miles from the flat but, interestingly, only 17 miles from the Offa's Dyke footpath.

Hussein had found the house on Rightmove and, in what seemed to me an act of pure folly, the family had made a bid on it, and bought it. A few years ago they had purchased their council house in Tottenham for a knock down price. Hussein had noticed that prices in Tottenham were about twenty times dearer than rural North Wales, particularly since Spurs' huge new stadium development had gentrified the London borough. The family had taken advantage of this discrepancy by selling in one place and buying in the other. It was a very British move. But they had absolutely no idea of what Denbigh or North Wales was like. I had lived in the hills of Flintshire in the 90s and noughties so I knew.

To me, moving a family of Muslim, Somalian, British adults and children to Denbigh would have been a big deal **my sister went to a welsh uni and assured us that the people in North Wales are fine with everyone as long as you're not English**. Moving a family of Christian, white, English people from London to Denbigh would not be something I'd recommend without a lot of thought. Although a pretty town, unspoilt by shameful post-war development, facing south on the side of a hill at the end of the sublime Clywdian valley, Denbigh was nevertheless a fairly tough, unreconstructed Welsh county town. A lot of Welsh was spoken there. The people were not used to newcomers. The place had the look of a town which was not growing in size but shrinking, as its young occupants migrated outwards. I did not know their attitude to new arrivals, whether of English or African descent.

Hussein had been living in Denbigh for two months when I arrived to pick him up. I didn't miss going to Tottenham. The traffic was always bad.As I drove into Denbigh, I kept an eye out for brown or black people. Were Hussein's family the only Africans in the village? I didn't see any others, but I did see a neat and tidy provincial town, with people who looked busy and contented.

Hussein had off street parking in a courtyard behind a house that stood tall and handsome in the sunshine. The brood of kids that had scrambled over the sofa in Tottenham ran out of the back door in a pack to greet me. All five of them were half southern, half northern hemisphere children. That is, half white and half black. They ranged in ages from 3 to 9, and all joyously shouted *Grandpa!* when they saw me, despite only two of them being related to me, by my clearly outdated definition. **We've all been brought up to not call 'grown ups' by their names so it's either Grandpa or Uncle depending on age.**

My first instinct was to pick out my blood grandchildren and explain that I was Grandpa only to them, but after a moment thought, what the hell, these kids love calling me Grandpa and I quite like this feeling of having five beautiful, brown-eyed, caramel-skinned grandchildren mobbing me and tugging on my sleeves.

It was my first taste of the delights of an extended family. I had only ever been in a nuclear, Christian style one. Here was my blood. Here was my line. Here was my DNA heading off into the future, via the biscuit tin, on their little, sturdy toddler legs.

I asked where Hussein was, and was informed that he had a suite of rooms upstairs which the kids were only allowed into by invitation. *The prince is in residence,* I thought. They swarmed around me as we went to the door. The women were in the kitchen preparing a light snack of nuts, pastries and biscuits for me.

'So,' I said, 'how are you finding Denbigh?'

'It is very nice. The streets are clean, no syringes.' **We had two staircases in the block of flats we lived in – one was always covered in piss the other always had tin foil from burning heroin and I had seen a syringe one or two times. But the biggest worry was always the crime; a few weeks before we moved out, we had a shooting**

147

downstairs and no one called the police, and a few weeks before that we had a stabbing in the block.

'I bet you miss your friends in London?' I hadn't left the flat for about a year or two due to anxiety, and felt like throwing up every time going outside was mentioned. So, I hadn't met up with any of my mates for a year or two.

'It is good to be away from them,' answered Hussein's mum, she of the magic oil. 'Especially Somalis always looking in our business. Here we are more free to do what we want.' **The African aunties are forever judging.**

'How is the school here?'

'Very good. The best school is Welsh-speaking. So the boys go there and learn to speak Welsh.'

'Really?' I asked. 'They are taught in Welsh?'

'Yes. It is good for them to learn to speak Welsh.'

To them, Welsh was just the latest of a string of languages they had encountered on their journey from Mogadishu to Denbigh. Growing up in England in the 60s and 70s, I had been taught to be prejudiced and bigoted about the Welsh people and their language. I was told it was impossibly complicated and difficult to learn, so it was best banned. To hear the language spoken about in such neutral terms was a delightful novelty.

When Hussein appeared, he was wearing a gown and slippers though it was quite late in the day. We had tried to walk the week before but Hussein had been ill with a typically mysterious Hussein ailment: cold bones.

We left the five children standing ruefully at the door watching us leave, all waving sadly at Hussein, and drove through Wales back to Four Crosses. Looking for a place to park, we passed the garage where the lady had phoned the taxi for us.

'Do you remember that?' I said.

'Yes,' said Hussein, almost flinching at the memory.

I parked the car by the war memorial and looked around to see if we were being watched. I was particularly anxious about the car being stolen because I had a medical condition which was troubling me that morning. That was how anxiety worked for me. A worry about one thing popped up as an anxiety about something apparently (most would say completely) unconnected. A few weeks before, I had somehow managed to catch scabies skin mites, microscopic parasites that burrowed under the skin. As I closed the car door, I felt some mites moving on my arm. My arms and leg were covered in red itchy bumps some of which were weeping pus. I hadn't told Hussein about my affliction. **You told me later. Every time I hear about these scabies I get itchy.** They were too small to see, but the doctor had told me they were there. From time to time, they became impossibly, maddeningly itchy. Their *modus operandi* was, once under my skin, to leave eggs and poo there to rot. **Itchy AF right now.** There's a Goya etching of a man with scabies who has wild bulging eyes and hair standing on end. I came upon it on my trawl across the Internet for information on my parasite. I thought, *he looks like I feel.* I was ashamed to have scabies, a disease I associated with a lack of personal hygiene. It put me in a grim mood, but I did notice that it was strange that my skin was needing so much attention, in keeping with the whole project. Luckily, the doc had told me that an ointment called Lyclear would soon polish the microscopic blighters off, and I had smeared it all over me before we got started that morning.

We looked at the Cicerone Offa's Dyke Path 1:25,000 route map booklet and set off through the quiet village. Immediately, I sensed something had changed. Hussein was striding out ahead of me. Yes, striding. He had never strode before. And his body no longer possessed that huddled, cowed shape but was upright, and his gaze, instead of on his boots, was ranged across the flat valley. We came alongside the Monty again, but this time it was silted up and thick with reeds and grasses. We crossed a river at some sluices which looked modern, no doubt installed to try and stop the flooding of new housing estates built on the water meadows downstream. Overhead the cloud was quilted, but the day was still and warm. When I arrived at the aqueduct where the Monty crossed the River Vyrnwy, Hussein was impatiently waiting for me and turned to go.

'Hold on,' I said, 'I need a rest.' My back felt as though it was being pounded by a lump hammer with every step. If I leant forward to avoid the hammer it was like touching a 50-kilowatt cable.

'Oh. Okay,' said Hussein.

'Have you got fit?' I said.

'I walked around Mombasa every day,' he said. 'I really enjoyed it. It was good to be around black people, and, well ... no white people, going to the mosque five times a day.' He beamed a happy smile as he remembered these trips in the hot sunshine of Kenya. **It's nice to be around your people, people who look like you. So you're not being constantly being prejudged.**

I looked him up and down. 'You seem happier,' I said.

'Yeah. I am.'

'What do you think of Denbigh?'

'Terrible food, but good people. It's nice to have the space in the house.' **London is blessed with options when it comes to food, but not living space.**

'I'm pleased you've settled in. It's a bit of a miracle, really,' I said.

'Come on,' he said.

'Hold on.' I tried to uncorkscrew my back but the man with the lump hammer soon started up again.

'So, you're more positive?' I asked.

'Much!' he laughed.

'That's great,' I said, thinking, *maybe he will rejoin life, manage his phobias about travel, and get back to finish university.* 'Have you been making plans for the future?'

'Yes,' he replied.

'And thinking more about getting out of the house again?'

'Yeah. Sure.'

'You're bright, Hussein. You need to go back to uni and finish your degree. You have a lot to contribute to the world. Britain needs people like you. Badly.'

He grunted. I thought, *he is absorbing my wise and kind words, but doesn't like to admit it.* I didn't blame him. It must be annoying to be lectured by me.

'Tell me about Somalia,' I said, when the path widened enough to walk side by side.

'I been in Kenya, Guy,' he sighed.

'I know, but Somalia is where you are really from.'

'I've never been there.'

'Come on. It's your heritage. Tell me a little about it. Incredibly, we're not taught about the Horn of Africa at school here. I know you'll find that hard to believe.'

'Somalia had a civilisation on a level with Egypt.[1] It was right up there with the Roman Empire. But white people suppressed it. It ruled over north east Africa and the Arabian Peninsula. It was rich and built beautiful buildings. You've seen the churches, right? That stone one in the big hole in the ground? Hand carved. All of it. Somali has the most UNESCO sites in the whole of Africa. Two more than Egypt, bro.'

'You don't have so many tourists because of your tendency to kidnap them. Quite cheap to go to Somalia but 5 million quid to leave.'

'Very funny. Somalia was important in all religions of the middle east: Judaism, Christianity and Islam. The Queen of Sheba came from Somalia. They say the Ark of the Covenant is hidden there in some church, though I bet if it was it's been nicked by some white European imperial power. In Islam, the first Muslims fled to Somalia where they were given refuge. It was a great kingdom. Civilised and cultured. We were good people.'

We skirted the edge of a golf course and another disused quarry, but then the land turned wild as we headed into the mountains of Wales. There, the country seemed beyond taming, with scruffy woods and wind-blown moorland. It was limestone geology, with rushing rivers, cliffs and little mossy waterfalls. It felt like bandit country where man's writ was not so strong.

Hussein continued to make the pace out ahead with a spring in his step **proof that the Mumma's oil works**

---

[1]When I checked Hussein's claims I found they stood up – if you include Ethiopia in his definition of Somalia. This is reasonable because the border is a modern European creation that post-dates all of the stuff he refers to.

and I hoped he was thinking, as I was, how beautiful and varied the landscape of Britain was.

I bit back the pain and caught up with him.

'Maybe I could come to Africa next time you go and do a walk there.'

'Where?'

'We could walk across the place your family lived, in Somalia.'

'I don't think so, Guy. They got Sharia law there, remember. I think I said they've got terrorists, and pirates. And I don't think you'd last a day in any country that practised Islamic Sharia. You'd have to give up all your bad habits.'

'So? I come in peace,' I said.

'They will kill you,' he said.

'Okay,' I said and fell behind again.

There was nowhere to stop for lunch, so we walked on, with me getting further behind, or finding ways to slow Hussein down till a misty dusk fell when we were on heathland. To add to the mystery, a large black dog loped out of the thicket towards us. Later we met a shrill woman who said, 'Have you seen my dog?' in a suspicious tone as if we were planning to steal it. We told her where it had gone and she disappeared into the mist after it. I looked at the map; we were on an old racecourse.

The path went through a sandy wood where the roots veined the ground. I had necked a handful of painkillers and my mind was cloudy. If deracinate means to uproot, did the word race come from the latin radix, for root? It started to worry me, because we can't do anything about our roots, we can only do things with our leaves, and branches. It was a problem. I asked for another stop and Hussein said, 'It's not far to the road, Guy.'

I Googled the etymology of the word race as I walked along, using it as an excuse to slow down. Race was nothing to do with root. It was race as in race course, or flow, like a mill race where the water rushes in a torrent. So, race was about the present, not the past.

'That's a relief,' I said.

'Come on,' said Hussein. 'It's getting dark.'

I looked at the Cicerone booklet to see if the path came back onto the tarmacked lane, because rough ground was becoming impossible for my back. Someone was holding a bayonet to my kidney and liver, jabbing it with a little twist every time I felt comfortable. A nerve the thickness of a bit of string seemed to have got caught between my hip bone and my pelvis and the only way to release it was to lean forward to the left and get the 50000 volt electric shock up my leg.

When Hussein put his arm around me for support, I found my eyes watering with pain and gratitude. We left the path and limped down a lane that looked about a mile long but felt like fifty, to a pub which, thank God, was open. If it hadn't been, I would have punched in the window and hurled myself through it. I asked for a quadruple whisky and tried not to cry while Hussein ate his crisps.

# 16.

Torrential rain fell the next morning, but it was going to be our last day walking. So I didn't care a toss. We were going to get to the finish line, a house just to the north of Llangollen, within range of a single good day's walking. And a lot of it was along another canal, which would be fast ground.

I literally crawled out of bed, essayed some stretches with my face on the bedroom carpet, and counted out my pain killers. My skin mites were really bad, and were now all over my legs and back, so I rubbed in an extra tube of Lyclear cream to take the attack to them. As I wrestled to reach my back without getting the 50,000 volt electric shock in my leg, I heard a report on the radio about the Italian government locking people in their homes because of some kind of infectious disease. I laughed. I scoffed at the uselessness of the Italians, a people who obviously had no idea how to run a country.

I remember everyone going on about how it was just the Italians. 'They've got an ageing population and a government that doesn't work', and I just sat by and listened while Googling and comparing the demographics of Italy and the UK. And looking at how many ventilators we had per 100,000. Spoiler: Italy had more vents and we've got a similar age breakdown to Italy, but I stayed seated, shaking my head on the inside and thinking *these people have too much confidence in our own government and how well run it is*.

We took up where we had left the path, walking on boggy ground into diagonal rain. The path didn't usually cross wet ground. Offa had been able to choose the best terrain. I was just thinking this when I checked the map to see we had gone wrong. We retraced our steps and simultaneously saw a raised bump with old stones by it under a grove of oaks.

'Offa,' we said together.

'Why don't they make more films in Wales?' Hussein, being conversational, asked.

'I don't know,' I croaked.

'They should make the tax breaks more attractive. That's how you attract international productions. Is that hurting?'

'Yes, a lot.'

'You need Mumma's oil for it.'

'I doubt it very much.'

'Mumma's oil is good for bones and for skin and for liver. It worked on me. Do you remember how slow I used to be?' **After this book I might just have to market this oil.**

He was bouncing along in a chatty mood. **I've found my slogan: 'Bounce along with Mumma's oil', though I might have to change the name. I would use 'bounce along with Africa oil', but Africa doesn't really sell stuff in England. That's racism.** I was trying to hold my body and mind together to get me to the end. The rain eased, but the water had got through my jacket into my jersey and trousers. I felt like I was steaming. I think my feet made a noise.

At Chirk Castle I saw from the map that the old path had been heavily diverted (and annoyingly lengthened) to avoid the castle, which still functioned as a residence. I guess it was done by the man who lived there, probably in the 70s, when he noticed the path getting busier. He would have called in his estate manager, 'For God's sakes get that ruddy right of way moved, it's unconscionable how the riff raff drag themselves past the windows, gawping in.'

'But you have given the castle to the National Trust, sir,' the manager would remind his boss.

'That's just on paper, I still own it. Get that path moved, ruddy ramblers.'

What had looked, at first glance, like an hour's walk through the castle grounds turned out to be a two-hour detour out to the kennels, around an old saw mill and back down a secondary drive, the castle a mile away to our right at all times. The original path was actually marked on the map in the booklet by a thick blue line, as if to remind walkers of the injustice. That blue line evinced fury, as though it was drawn by a cartographer who knew the old and correct position of the path and was annoyed having to mark its modern line, away from the castle. It was a statement saying *we have not forgotten where we used to be allowed to walk, and we will walk that way again after the revolution which will be led not by the miners and ship workers but by the Ramblers Association.*

The day brightened, the rain eased and then stopped, and we made okay speed down the drive away from the castle, but I needed a rest. A Land Rover pulling a game cart dangling with dead pheasants swept us on to the verge.

'There's a shoot going on,' I said to Hussein.

Fifteen minutes later, when we were walking by a field under a wood, I saw three people with dogs and guns come through a gate and move onto the numbered pegs standing in the wet turf.

'Let's stop here and watch a drive,' I said. We were on the tarmac of a neat bungalow, looking over a cut winter hedge. The leafless branches and twigs of a birch, oak and ash wood reached up the hill to the horizon. A couple of old oaks grew from hedges that ran down the sides of the hill. The composition of the wood, the guns, their dogs—the browns, greens, blacks and greys, was painterly. We were watching an ancient scene. The rich people out at their sport, shooting game on a winter's day. Two curious strangers had stopped to watch them from the road. Hussein and I. The clouds had thinned to patches of misty blue sky. Hussein shivered as it grew cold now that we were standing still.

'What are they doing?' He asked.

'Shooting pheasants,' I said. The gun in front of us was a woman. She had a dark spaniel at her feet. She unsleeved her gun. 'It's probably the last day's shooting of the season, so there won't be many birds. Hence the woman. Most of the birds are dead or too pissed off to fly any more to make it fun. Some shoots have cocks-only days at the end of the season, to build the myth that the hens should be conserved to breed, but there is no breeding going on around here. The new pheasants are bought in as poults and released into the woods. It's a death camp for pheasants.'

'I'd like to try that,' Hussein said.

'I can see you in plus fours, Hunters, shooting jacket and tweed cap,' I said. 'I don't know if you'd be able to hit anything with a gun though.'

158

'I'm black and from Tottenham, Guy, we're famous for it.' Or that's how it seems to most people outside of London – we're all armed with knives and guns having shoot outs on a daily basis. Especially that year when everyone was going crazy about the stabbings in London. I remember saying that shit used to be a lot worse eight to ten years ago, when we used to have a police helicopter hovering over our secondary school every day after school and at least two police horses and the occasional van load of officers.[1]

'Let's stay and watch. The people in the field are waiting for the beaters who are at the top of the hill now but will comb slowly through the wood making a lot of noise to scare the pheasants who have been lured in there with food, making them fly out on this side, where they will be shot at.'

'What's that man with the flag doing?'

'That's an underkeeper, standing out to the side of the wood to stop the birds escaping in that direction and not over the guns. The flag is made of a thick plastic fertliser bag, that's why it makes such a crack when he flaps it.'

We began to hear the whistles and shouts and tapping of the beaters entering the wood at the top, faintly at first and then louder. Our senses were cocked. And I felt the anticipation as the whistles and calls came closer through the wood.

---

[1]And you told me that you were never on the receiving end of any racial abuse. Being buzzed by the cops when you're a kid is racial abuse.

Suddenly, some shouts turned into louder yelps and hoots, and we heard the klaxon call of a pheasant and the rattling flapping of its wings as it rose from the trees.

'It's high,' I said.

The bird worked its wings a few more times and then glided towards the guns. Hussein and I watched it until it crumpled in the air and then we heard the bang of the gunshot as it tumbled to ground.

It was a supremely British scene, for all its flaws. And it was my impression that Hussein was enjoying it. He watched closely and asked what was going on. He saw the dogs running to retrieve the birds, heard the beaters shouting in Welsh, and stared at the dead birds in the game cart when it passed us going in the opposite direction.

It was afternoon when we left the shoot and I limped behind Hussein down a long hill to the Llangollen canal — another really beautiful example of canal engineering. It ran along the edge of hills, under cliffs, and through tunnels to connect this corner of Wales to England. We still had at least 7 miles until our finish line, and Hussein wanted to go for it, even though it would mean we would arrive after dark. Every step was searing agony for me but I thought I could do it.

'Are you all right, Guy? I'm worried, man, that looks painful.'

I stopped and grimaced. 'It is painful, Hussein, but this expedition will not fail.'

'Oh,' he said. 'I thought it was going to.'

'Have you ever heard of Captain Scott of the Antarctic? He was the leader of an expedition to the North Pole. In 1911. 1911,' I said again. 'What a year to have been alive and to be British. Just before the First

World War, when the flower of our youth was so cruelly mown down. By the Germans. Never forget that. You've heard of the First World War, I take it?'

'You often mention it, Guy.' **The time Europe's royal families—who were at this point all related—couldn't get along and decided to get the rest of the world involved, killing millions of young common folks in what was essentially a family disagreement.**

'Scott's expedition was a famous British achievement. It became a legend of national identity. However bad conditions got, and they ran out of food and fuel in punishingly cold weather, they never gave up and they never let their spirits flag. That is the kind of leader I want to be.'

'Did Captain Scott make it in the end?'

'He was a bloody brave man, and he led a courageous team.'

'Oh.'

'That's you, Hussein.'

'I think you should sit down, Guy,' he said, pointing to a tree trunk.

I just wanted to get it over and done with and get this book, for what it was worth, off to the publishers. The fact is that, although Hussein dragged me to Llangollen like he dragged me to understanding, I feared that nobody else white and English was going to be interested in our friendship. Gammon and samosa. My head was full of gloomy and negative thoughts as I trudged wonkily behind Hussein, counting the yards off in my mind. It was a good eleven squares on the map, and some of them were horribly wrinkled with contours. Both up or down, anything steep was agony for me. My mouth was dry. Imagine a live nerve in a stone mortar. Now grind it with a pestle until it grunted and squeaked. That was going on in the socket of my pelvis with a variant of it in a couple of lower vertebrae. My skin was raw and fiery. I just wanted to sit down. I just wanted to sit down.

'What?' Hussein said.

I must have said it out loud. 'Nothing,' I said.

'Do you need to sit down?'

'In a bit,' I said. 'I'll be all right.'

We were approaching one of the most impressive aqueducts in the world, a UNESCO World Heritage Site, where the canal was suspended 200 feet over the River Dee on a spectacular set of towering brick arches. The canal straightened up as it linked with the aqueduct, which was constructed of wrought iron and cut stone, with no concrete, in 1795. Strong but delicate, imaginative but functional (it was still working fine 250 years later) crossing it was definitely going to be one of the highlights of the walk. The path predated the aqueduct by centuries, and so it went down into the vale and crossed the wide and impressive Dee river on a medieval stone bridge which still stood. The purist path walker took the oldest line, but I said to Hussein, 'we'll go over the aqueduct and join the path on the other side. It's what most walkers do.'

I squeezed past a yellow council sign that said Canal Closed for Maintenance.

'I think it's closed, Guy,' Hussein said.

'For barges, for boats, but the footpath will be open.'

I limped the five hundred yards to the start of the bridge. My mites were swarming across my back and I kept feeling them at the nape of my neck. I wanted to stop then and there and empty a tube of the cream onto my skin.

We still had 7 miles to go after the aqueduct. I summoned the memory of Shackleton and Mallory and pushed on to the summit with Hussein, now my Sherpa, at my side.

'You may have to carry me the last three miles,' I said to Hussein.

History does not record his reply. **Probably, 'you can sit there while I try find phone signal for a taxi to come pick us up'.**

When we finally reached the aqueduct there was another sign, this one saying NO BOATS NO PEDESTRIANS. On the bridge, two men in high viz jackets and white plastic hard hats were banging a nail into a length of 2 by 4. There was plenty of room to pass them safely so I started to squeeze round the signs.

'Come on, I'm not going back,' I said. 'Follow me.'

Hussein stood still. I went through the gap and the men looked up. One waved his arm.

'No entry. Closed,' he said.

'But we are on the Offa's Dyke Path walk,' I said. 'Surely it's okay to walk across it.'

'Sorry. No entry.'

'Well how do I get over?'

'You turn round, go back to the lagoon, and take the road down to the old bridge and walk back up the other side.'

I felt a sharp jet of pure anger spurt up against this horrible little man in his yellow jacket. I had to vanquish this jobsworth.

'You racist!' I was about to shout, but just resisted it. We turned round. As I hobbled back up to the lagoon I said quietly to Hussein 'They were racist bastards weren't they? Didn't you think?'

He said, 'Honestly, Guy, that's a bad thing to say, bro.'

'Yeah. I'm not well, I'm sorry,' I said.

'I don't think you're strong enough to walk the last stretch,'

'Really?' I said.

'I know you want to be Captain Scott. But times have changed. We live in more relaxed days. It doesn't matter if we don't make it tonight, bro. We can finish it off another time.'

'Dear God,' I shuddered. 'When will it ever end?'

'We'll get there,' he said.

'We must,' I said.

'But this evening, let's just get into that town, however you say it, and find a taxi. You think they've got Uber? We can come back in a few days when you're feeling better.'

'It's not very Captain Scott.' I said.

'Yeah, but didn't he die?' Hussein said. 'Well, we don't want that, do we?'

Dusk started falling and Hussein walked me three miles down the tow path into the little town. I remember passing under one bridge that had a sign saying Llangollen was 2 miles ahead. We walked past probably three or four more bridges before we saw the next sign and we looked up hoping to see it saying Llangollen 1 or 0.5 miles ahead but it said something like 1.6 miles away. And we stood their laughing for a minute or two in pain. We were too far from the road to call a taxi so I just had to foot slog it. I would not have made it without Hussein. Over the course of about half an hour I had changed from Robert Falcon Scott to Captain Oates. The skin mites were coming down my sleeves onto my wrists and up my shirt onto my neck so I kept having to stop and brush the horrible things off. And my nerve ending had swollen to the size of a grape which was being slammed in a cupboard door every time I took a step. I looked at the still water of the canal and thought, just fall in, Guy. Then someone'll drag you out and maybe put you in an ambulance, where you belong. **This is the feeling I used to have when driving up to North Wales from London, always felt like opening the doors and just jumping out of the moving car.**

The sky darkened above me, and the branches and trees turned to silhouettes, growing sinister. The path was deserted but we came to a barge with smoke coming out of a chimney and a man on the bank carving, from blocks of pine, some really ugly sculptures of fat owls and improbable birds of prey which I stopped to scowl at.

'Come on,' I felt Hussein pull my arm. 'Not far to go now ... come on.' I wanted to hold him for support and for friendliness but couldn't because I was worried my skin mites would jump onto him. After walking 20 yards he was 18 yards ahead. I hobbled, I shuffled, I limped behind him, tugged by his encouraging words and patient kindness. Eventually, after one of the hardest hours of my life, I saw the lights of the town of Llangollen twinkling through the wood.

As we were both famished, we hobbled down the high street to a kebab shop. They only had a formica shelf to sit on, but I placed my bum on it as if it were deeply upholstered chesterfield sofa. I looked at the kebab guys and they gave me an encouraging smile. I worked out why. I was with Hussein, so they were confident I wouldn't racially abuse them.

At the Spar I leant half dead against a pillar while Hussein politely asked the checkout woman if she would call us a cab. He then led me outside, my carer.

# 17.

I had to rest for a week at home before I was able to stand up from sitting down in under five minutes. I couldn't believe we'd stopped a couple of miles short of the finish line. I made an appointment to see the doctor, who sent me to a dermatologist as an emergency patient, a concept I never knew existed.

She was a young Spanish woman who told me to undress. She came up close to my skin, tutted and said, 'Oh no. That is not right,' which made me smile, because it was not something one would normally say about someone's skin. 'Tell me, what have you been doing?' she asked.

I said, 'I've had scabies and I cannot get rid of them no matter how much cream I put on...'

'What ointment are you using?'

I took the tube from my pocket. She glanced at it, and then went back to my arm.

'How much have you put on?' she said.

'Twice a day recently, but it doesn't seem to be working,' I said.

She picked up a magnifying glass and inspected my stomach and back.

Then she said, 'This isn't scabies. I don't think you ever had scabies. This is simply poisoning from the Lyclear ointment which you are not meant to use more than twice a year because it's so toxic. Didn't you read the instructions?'

'What?'

She took off her glasses. 'You can get dressed now,' she said. 'This is self-inflicted. You've been doing it to yourself. Just stop putting on the ointment and you'll get better. If you don't, come and see me again.'

I paid her, went outside and stood watching the London traffic, wondering if there was something metaphorical to say, or understand, about my skin. Worrying about it had made it worse, because I had upped the wrong treatment. That didn't work. Ignoring the race problem has considerably exacerbated it. I turned the subject over in my head looking for the metaphor. After a minute of thought I came to the conclusion that my condition was nothing to with race or racism. It was a manifestation of my own unconnected idiocy.

The chiropractor, a petite 70-year-old woman with short blond hair and a ballroom dancing habit laid me out on her massage table like a run over slinky. She said, 'Well what have you been up to?'

I gave my usual response. 'Nothing much.'

'You feel tense, and anxious. I know you have a tendency to internalise all those difficult emotions, don't you?'

'I don't have any difficult emotions,' I said.

She smiled.

'There's a lot of conflict here,' she said, 'and anxiety.'

While she cracked my vertebrae and stretched my muscles I said, 'I have been on this walk with my kind of son-in-law who's African by birth **and heritage, please,** and I've learnt a lot about how racist this country is. And kind of, maybe, a bit how I might be. And I was hoping I could show him enough to give us a second, or in his case probably a fifty-third chance, so that's the project I've been on.' I sighed as she did something with my leg that released something between my shoulder blades.

She pressed on a knot of muscle, 'there is a lot here,' she said.

I thought, *she's putting the cat on the roof for another six sessions at fifty quid a pop.* I said, 'I have been surprised by how Hussein is treated, and it's made him feel negative about the way he thinks about Britain. I feel bad about it. You know, personally.' And I went on to talk about race in the UK and felt myself slowly losing the room.

Her, 'Yes,' and, 'I know it's terrible,' faded to, 'mmm', and tuts. There is a book called *Why I'm No Longer Talking to White People About Race* – and it's by a black woman called Reni Eddo Lodge. It's even worse trying to talk to a white person about race if you, too, are white.

I rang Hussein. 'We better put a date in the diary to finish the walk.'

'Is your back okay?'

'It's not great, but I don't think it's going to totally be cured, maybe ever, but it's okay. I want to walk.'

'What about this virus thing?'

'This flu? What about it?' I asked.

'I think that we may be stopped moving about the country. It could be illegal for you to travel to Wales, I heard,' Hussein said.

'Don't be ridiculous. For a start it's nothing but a heavy cold, and second, mark my words, there is no British government who could ever, conceivably, stop an Englishman using the Queen's highway in his country to go absolutely wheresoever he wishes.'

'I heard they are going to lockdown whole cities.'

'Hussein you are so credulous. Stop thinking we don't have rights. It's not Kenya or some tinpot African dictatorship, or China, where they treat their citizenry like vermin. This is Britain.'

'They locked down Italy.'

'Italy? Let me give you a clue about the governance of Italy. Do you know what side they fought on in the Second World War?'

'Guy, not the war again?'

'Listen. The Italians fought on both sides. That's a clue. The French did too, it's worth mentioning. It basically means they don't know their ass from their elbow. The Brits, mark my words, will not fall into the same trap.'

'Well, I heard it might happen.'

'Let's meet after the weekend. Tuesday, ok? I'll come and pick you up. Don't you worry. Be ready to roll.'

I didn't see Hussein for seventeen weeks. Everything fell away.

The chiropractor went into retirement, the restaurants faded away, and the streets fell silent as Glastonbury emptied. Sometimes I drove down the High Street in mid-morning and saw two people walking past shuttered shops like the town was dry heaving. Then friends faded away, neighbours withdrew, and even strangers deserted me. I was becalmed in those beating hot days of April and May in the year of COVID-19. We were shaken, but strangely still. All was confusion, but all was also somehow so simple. Up in the morning, look at the garden, fail to write this book for up to six hours at a time. I was worried about the world in this sorrowful time.

I looked at the daily diary I kept, in which I marked each day of the 93 day lockdown. On day 5, I wrote: *This is absolutely intolerable, and cannot last more than 48 hours. No population can take this treatment. I predict with absolute certainty an uprising within a week.*

On day 55, I wrote: *The first three hours of my day usually go well, and then it all starts to fall apart. I'm not sure why. Is it because I am tired out after three hours of pottering about? Jesus Christ. Or is it that I sense the futility of life and quietly give up? Only with a series of naps can I manage to get to 6pm and a drink, which gets me through to dinner after which I have only thought: bed.*

Through all of this I was sitting at home, fairly calm, one of the few who was probably used to the new reality because of those two years' worth of experience in staying at home and not socialising when I was still in London. Now I was doing it in a bigger house, and Mum didn't have to go to work, so maybe lockdown worked out well for me and the family. We thanked God we weren't still in a three bedroom flat on the fourth floor with what felt like twenty kids. Instead, we now lived in a detached house with a garden meaning the kids could run around and be noisy in the house, and when it became too much, we could kick them out for the day into the garden with their scooters and bikes.

Day 63, my diary was a portrait of a dissolving mind: *All we can opinion to another, depending on who's on the radio, I am of the view this minute that* the middle-aged should stop holding the country to ransom. My finger nails have grown for the first time in fifty years. What is that about? I'm a lifer on the wing meekly going along with arrangements, like a cow tied in a stall.

# 18.

Every day of lockdown I got out this manuscript and stared at it. I thought I had a subject of importance, but my momentum slowed when I realised how uninterested people – white ones particularly – were in the subjects of race, nationality and justice. Would the world ever wake up to the hugeness of racism? Would they see that it was the biggest pollutant on the planet, way in front of carbon dioxide? At least carbon dioxide was an equal opportunities killer. But, like many writers, I started wondering if there were any other subjects left to write about in 2020 apart from the sodding virus and mass lockdown.

I listened to talk radio all day long, being alternatively maddened and soothed until I was exhausted. We all tried to understand what was going on and predict what was going to happen. It was a verbal stream of Covid, for hours and hours, with no other story, until one sunny, dry morning, as I stared at a pheasant prancing across the lawn, I heard the report on the news of a black man in Minneapolis killed by a cop. The policeman knelt on his neck for 7 minutes and 46 seconds during arrest. Quite a lot has changed since I heard that first report on my lockdown desert island. One of the things is how

I would now write that first sentence. I would now say George Floyd was the man the white cops killed, not the black man killed by the cops. **I know that's what people are saying now, but I think *black man killed by the cops* is probably more appropriate because the problem is with the institution itself – it just so happens to be full of poorly trained and educated white people and some black people.**

Over the next few days, the footage of the murder, shot from different angles on different phones and cameras, went viral and ended up on my laptop. I watched it in stunned, shamed silence. I thought of Hussein, immediately. I looked at that stupid, swaggering policeman and thought, *you are disgrace to humanity. How have you dropped so low?*

Because the early footage was shot from the pavement where the bystanders were told to stand back, George was small in the frame where he lay on the road by the back wheel of the police car, but no less powerful. Any fictional movie would have gone to a close-up, but there were no close-ups for days, until the body cams worn by the police were released. The lack of a close-up meant I had to lean in and look closely at the most important part of the screen, and this made it more real. It wasn't some bullshit movie.

I thought, *what am I going to say to Hussein?* The cop, Derek Chauvin, had eighteen complaints about his conduct as a policeman, but had still been sent out on patrol. When the cop cams were eventually released you could feel the swagger in him from the movement of the camera and the alarm on the faces of the ordinary citizens when he approached.

174

Chauvin got into a fight with George, and then called some other cops and, with their help, held George down on the ground. The brutality was premeditated. It was payback for struggling with him earlier and I bet a hundred other bullshit resentments rattling round Chauvin's racist skull. I urge all white people to fully denounce Chauvin. He was the kind of man that is bringing us all into disrepute. He tried to plea bargain a third-degree murder charge which would have seen him back on the streets and, God knows, knowing America, probably back in uniform within five years. But the upsurge of fury made the prosecutors drop that idea and charge him with second-degree murder two days later. If they find he did have intention, which to me is an open and shut case, he will get life for first-degree murder.

One of the other cops on the scene was a rookie on his third day called Thomas Lane. **This, for me, strengthened the idea that it's not just white cops, but the institution itself that looks at every black man as a potential threat and probably something to do with the American public and media who often find excuses for the murder. Usually, as soon as a story comes out about a black man shot, I always wait to see what excuse they'll make, its usually, 'oh he had a criminal record'.** He looked so lost and confused. It was his third day as a policeman, and this. He is now an ex-cop. Not an illustrious career. He stood and kept bystanders on the pavement while George howled, '*I can't breathe, I can't breathe*'. And, heartbreakingly, '*Mumma! Mumma! I love you,*' just before he began his steep descent to silence and death.

175

I only saw the bystanders properly on this young cop's bodycam as he stood trying to block the view of the murder so people couldn't record it on their phones. Of the six bystanders who stopped to remonstrate with Chauvin, three were white, all young women. I was relieved finally to see some white people who were not acting like complete inhuman shits.

I was glad I was stuck in Glastonbury and not walking past Cup Foods on Chicago Avenue in Minneapolis that Monday afternoon at the end of May, because I do not know if I would have had the guts and presence of mind to stand with those young women, lift up my phone and shout at the cop who was killing George. You can see quite a few people did just walk on by, turning their heads to look and then getting on their way, minding their own business. I fear that would have been me. The most articulate of the remonstrators was a young black man with a T-shirt on that said NORTHSIDE BOXING CLUB. All were heroes on that sidewalk, but he was the leader. He kept up a running monologue haranguing the police.

'He ain't resisting arrest right now, bro! He's not responsive now. Check on him, bro! Check his pulse, bro!' Forced, I imagine, out of fear for his own life to call a viperous murderer 'bro' to protect himself from arrest and a beating of his own.

'Get off his fucking neck, bro!' The shouting increased. The black and white folks were equally angry. Thank God for that. **The saddest part for me was hearing this 46-year-old man crying out for his dead mum, as he was being killed.**

I watched George Floyd lying still. He was dead. It had happened with all of us watching, admittedly me later and at a distance, but I saw it and could not deny it.

It was too strong for lots of white folk. Just too much of an obvious injustice for them to swallow. I was amazed at in the comments section under the video on YouTube. White people started saying the footage was fake. That George was a mannequin. That the whole thing was staged in psy ops scheme. *Floyd died 3 years ago*, one wrote, a person unable to accept the fact that brutal racist murders perpetrated by cops on the street went completely unchecked.

I sat in the baking heat of late-May lockdown weather. The entire country becalmed.

*Now*, I thought, *what business have I to write about it?* I was a white middle-aged, middle class Englishman and I lived 4000 miles east of Cup Foods, Minneapolis.

I thought *here we go again*, let's wait for the character assassination, followed by some twitter hashtag saying #justice4 *insert name here*, a few comments from the democrats, saying this is bad, a few comments from republicans saying let's wait to see the full picture, the local AG refuse to prosecute or they do this thing where they put on a show and pretend they're going to do something, and they just sit on it hoping the noise goes down and rule that no further action will be taken. So, I expected very little to happen and had zero hope of any change.

I had a lump in my throat. Not a tear in my eye, but a burning anger. And I knew why. It was now personal. I could picture not just Hussein lying on the tarmac with that pig of a man kneeling on his neck, but I could see my family, my beautiful grandson and granddaughter and all my adopted grandchildren, my blood, with their necks under the knee, by the back offside wheel of that police car. My grandkids were about to grow up on the wrong end of the racial deal. It may sound selfish that I only became motivated at the age of sixty-three because my grandchildren were half African, but I don't care. It's better to have a bad reason for doing the right thing than never to do it at all. I now had skin in the game, and the gloves were off as far I was concerned.

I swore to myself then never to be someone who walked on by, minding my own business. I would stand on the pavement and shout. I had had enough. You cannot rely on me to be quiet. Not anymore.

I spoke to Hussein.

'I'm afraid it's total lockdown in Wales,' he said. 'No walking.'

'Really? Look, we've only got a few miles to do, and I want to get the book out and our story told.'

'A few miles?' Hussein repeated. 'That could take you five hours.'

'I'm much better now, thank you.'

'Well, we have to wait, the people are tough in Wales. We don't want you outsiders.'

I laughed.

'I'm serious. They are beating English tourists up.' He did not sound in the least bit sympathetic, I must report. 'You could get hurt.' **They weren't beating English tourists up, just turning them around and kicking them back over the border.**

'And you?'

'Oh no. I'm Welsh now, bro! I have an address in the principality.'

I thought, *he liked telling me that.*

'Ok. Hey,' I said, 'did you see that George Floyd footage?'

'I did, Guy.'
'What did you think?'
'I thought it wasn't very nice.'
'No. It was shocking. It made me feel sick.'
Hussein said nothing.

# 19.

After Minneapolis, St Paul was set ablaze for five consecutive nights, and around the world 14 million people demonstrated in 2000 cities and 60 countries, I began to worry that my manuscript had slightly underestimated the fury against us white people. I felt like this only happened because it was 2020. With the lockdown, no sports, no concerts or holidays and, for many, protesting was probably the first time they'd been out since the start of lockdown. And people were forced to sit down and watch this clip of a man being killed for eight minutes, not the usual five shots in the back or being shot while in bed, because usually people came up with 'the police feared for their lives' excuse. But this time the man was on the ground, crying for his mum, and slowly dying, and to top it off the police made no effort to check for a pulse. The paramedics who came after nine minutes put him on the stretcher and into the ambulance and once again didn't even bother checking for a pulse. It felt like they thought, or knew, that they could get away with it, and why not? They'd been getting away with it for over a century. They'd long learnt that black lives didn't matter.

I had been merrily splashing around in the shallows of racial politics and suddenly found myself upended by a corkscrew current and dragged downwards into deep and, frankly, scary water. I re-read the early chapters and began to soften some of my remarks, making them a little bit … what? A little more acceptable, I guessed, I hoped. I was worried that readers would metaphorically do to me what rioters had done to downtown Minneapolis. There was an exchange with Hussein early on in proceedings about how British colonialism taught good table manners to Africans which now made me wince. I thought, will everyone understand I was being ironic? But then I stopped myself, and undid all the changes. This was no time to be minimising the problem.

By early June, after weeks of beating sun and no rain, the lawn in front of my house was brown, and the flowerbeds were almost audibly moaning for water. The riots were followed by the arrival on our TVs and radios of new voices telling us how angry they were.

White people were in a muddle. We didn't know what to do and we certainly didn't know what to say. But most of the people – not all – wanted to say and do the right thing. We all quickly learnt, amongst other things, that you never said all lives matter. The ALL in that was like the ALL in the US Constitution's 'All men are created equal', when the guy who wrote it, Thomas Jefferson, owned 400 slaves.

We were rapidly doing a BA in being human in a racist landscape, but fortunately I had done a foundation course with Hussein. Working out what to do about it, I discovered, was harder. Should I go and march? I was not a marcher. Would that be enough if I did haul my ass to Trafalgar Square? **No! Marching becomes a thing** you just do to become cool amongst your friends, if it's all you do.[1] You can do marching, along with something else, for example marching and volunteering at an inner-city youth centre, or putting pressure on politicians to look at certain legislation, or look at certain systemic failures and see if you can help change them. Or with you, Guy, I'd say take your skills and go put in a shift at a school teaching them how you go from just a storyteller to a published author, or actively look for black, talented writers and help them get published. So marching isn't enough. You have to pair it up with something else. Enough with the performances, take action.

I guess I am marching with Hussein, and pairing it up with writing this book. Our walk along the Offa's Dyke Path was a march for Black Lives Matter. Of course it was. We just didn't name it so at its inception. But ours had the same aims, more or less. Just instead of 500,000 people, there were two of us, and we walked a bit slower.

I soon noticed loads of black and brown actors popping up in adverts. Way more frequently than their 13% of the non-white population. More than one in seven. I discussed this earlier in the book before I was aware of BLM. The sixty-year-old white man who used to greet me on my Bank Of Scotland home page, dressed, for some bizarre reason, as a Viking, was quickly swapped for a black guy with a good dark skin and round glasses leaning back on a sofa with a mug on the coffee table. I preferred the new image. The Viking had looked dour and dependable – the reliable guardian of my money. This new man looked relaxed and happy,

[1]That stings.

sort of saying *Don't worry, Guy, there's plenty of dough here for everyone.*

He was followed by a proliferation of brown people selling a plethora of products, all over the media I looked at, although I never saw any of them flogging anything associated with camping, climbing or rambling – all of which was still, firmly, white people shit.

After the corporations got in a flat panic and rammed their companies into reverse to essay a hasty U-turn, or at least a three-point turn, for some still took six weeks to get a black skinned person into their campaign, **companies acted like they'd only just learnt racism existed, as if it was the first time they'd seen images of a black man being killed** I heard a white person comment on the number of black people in adverts. It was a journalist friend, a hard bitten and entertaining old mucker of mine. I said my favourite advert was for an expensive hybrid Mercedes that played with the idea that the owner, a young black man, had no right to be driving it. **He's the Weeknd, Guy. You don't recognise him?**[2] My journalist friend and I were alone having a drink.

He said, 'There's only work for black actors in TV commercials now.'

Thus, the white tribe tried to pull me back, tugging me away from the deep water of change, like a tide that

---

[2]Guy here: okay, my hand is up, I admit it, I did not know the man in the ad was The Weeknd, one of the biggest stars in the music world. My editor, Miranda, and Hussein piled in on that. I decided not to change my remark in the interest of authenticity. The ad reads differently if you don't recognise him. I humbly suggest rather a lot of Mercedes' customers do not recognise The Weeknd.

carried me back to the beach where everything remained pretty much as it was. The white people, as ever, were on the beach. I didn't have to say anything. I did not have to say anything.

I did have to say something.

'These people have been traumatised,' I said. 'Hundreds of years of abuse. As a race they have PTSD. And they are in our family. They are in MY family! When someone in the family has a trauma – say a child falls in the swimming pool and can't swim – that's slavery, basically being drowned literally and metaphorically. You drag them out, but you don't just leave them on the side saying *you better just get on with it, you're fine now.*'

He took out his phone and scrolled it, I guessed to get up a statistic.

I continued, 'You wrap the kid in a towel, you give them sweet tea, you reassure them, you give them special care and attention, for a long time, to help them get over it. That's what putting them in all the ads is for me. That's what white people find hard to do ... why?'

He looked up from his phone. 'Oh right. Hey, I've got something funny to show you about Lionel Messi's father... look at this...'

Then there was the matter of the tree in my garden. My village friend, Ray the gravedigger, had told me years ago and repeated it often that a certain tall tree which stood in my garden had associations with the slave trade. Ray is a legend in these parts, with his long blond locks, lover-boy dialogue, stripped torso and rickety old Land Rover with, like its owner, a slightly dangling exhaust pipe.

'That were a sign you were in the slave trade,' he said. 'That tree. It's African, it is. They bought it back on the boat and planted it to show people in the olden days.'

It was certainly a different time when an association with the slave trade was something white people advertised. I knew enough about trees not to recognise it as indigenous, and after Ray informed me of its origin, I often looked at its layered branches and feathery leaves and pictured it on a dusty African plain. Every other year some delicate white flowers appeared right at the top, forty feet high. Out of reach of giraffes, I thought to myself.

With Black Lives Matter and the tectonic plates of race relations shifting underneath me, I started considering the tree again.

If anyone else knew of its association it could be embarrassing. No, it would have been embarrassing in 2018. In 2020 it was unacceptable. It was wonderful how fast the time was moving around race. A funny phrase that I wrote on page 24 of this book was dodgy by page 56 and unacceptable by 124. The tree which started as an oddity was now a billboard saying SLAVES BOUGHT AND SOLD HERE. It should come down. **There's no reason to cut it down.** Though interestingly there was a tree preservation order on it. It was now against the law to cut it down a tree with a preservation order on it, and the council tree man was not likely to give me a waiver. No one had ever asked for a TPO to be set aside on political, or social grounds, as I was proposing. It seemed so typically British that the state was going to step in and prevent me doing my bit to heal the racial wounds. **This is tokenistic bullshit, Guy. It wouldn't heal racial wounds and if anyone one suggested** it would, you should question it. You could always just use your capability to support projects in Africa or the Caribbean, tell your mates about the THE GREAT GREEN WALL project going on in Africa right now, which hopes to plant trees across the width of Africa, and, by doing so, providing employment, food security and reducing drought. As I said, Guy, enough with the performative gestures, and actually do something that will make a change. Cutting down the tree won't do anything, other than provide you with wood for burning during the winter – i.e. benefit you.

The most important thing for me was to finish the walk with Hussein, as soon as we were allowed to. That felt like an act of faith.

Getting me out of London and walking in the countryside, reducing my anxiety, seeing parts of the country I would have never ever thought about visiting, means a lot more than cutting down the tree.

# 20.

It was July when restrictions of movement were eased in England, though not in Wales, which as far as I could see had used the crisis to do what they had been wanting to do for years, which was ban the English from their fair country. **A nice change from Offa building the dyke to keep the Welsh out.** This meant that Hussein and I had to postpone the last couple of miles of the walk. It was characteristic, somehow, that the government managed to prevent me joining, in my way, the BLM movement.

Travel was permitted inside England and I left my house for the first time in ten weeks to see a friend in Chipping Norton, Gloucestershire.

He was renting, for the lockdown, the epitome of a British country house: a huge yet delicate Georgian mansion built of honey-coloured Cotswold stone, standing on the edge of a picture-perfect Cotswold village. From the lawn of the house, you looked down to a little river running into an ornamental lake and the rolling hills beyond.

I entered through the huge front door into a hall of chequered marble, and heard the guests gathered in the saloon. I use the word saloon because drawing-room or sitting-room did not quite do this magnificent, lofty space enough justice. Draped casually across sofa and fauteuils were the other members of the house party.

Perhaps because I had been writing this book in the weeks up to that day, I noticed quickly that there were two black people in the room, a woman and a man. I wasn't expecting it, I'll be honest. The black man was vaguely familiar, though I didn't know him. However, my record with remembering people was not good (although not as bad as an uncle by marriage who once, at a party, introduced himself to his second wife).

My host, a successful business man and social dynamo, took me aside and said, 'Guy, just to let you know that that guy on the sofa is the editor of ....' And he named a top fashion magazine, 'He's a cool man, so don't go and put your foot in it.'

I was about to say to my mate that he was now talking to the wokest 63-year-old he was ever likely to meet, but remembered it was not a competition, so just said I'd watch what I said.

The décor of the house was classic old-money, English upper class. The rug was Aubusson but it was worn to threads in front of the sofas, and the striped pink wall paper, though silk, looked like it was put up in the 80s. It was a relief compared to the blinged up interiors of the boutique hotels where everything was done up to the nines, effectively removing all traces of the country house look they were after.

I unpacked in my room and explored the house so as to delay having to face the guests since, after months on my own, I was feeling a bit shy. While wandering around I noticed, sitting on a console at the bottom of the curved staircase, a pair of busts of black men.

I decided to bring them up in conversation with the editor and his friend, a whip-smart woman called Trina, who was on his staff. This was the kind of thing I would never have done before I walked with Hussein.

'Did anyone notice those two heads on the table at the bottom of the stairs of black men?' I said. My host shot me a look of alarm. I was doing exactly what he had asked me not to, he thought.

Trina said, 'We don't like them.' She left open who exactly 'we' were. Was she talking just for her and Dan? I wanted to be in her group.

One of the other guests was a languid and well-educated aristocrat. I liked David very much. Do I need to say he was a person of no colour? Because now, when we read literature, we should not have to have all the black people pointed out in contrast to the white. Anyway, David was a white man. Are there any black British aristocrats? Hold on, I can think of one: Hussein.

**No hereditary title has been created for a black family. I Googled it.**[1]

The editor suggested, laughingly, that the statues should be thrown in the ornamental lake in the style of Mr Colston, the bronze slave trader from Bristol who ended up doing a low scoring dive into the water of the dock.

David looked up from the newspaper with an expression of fatigued annoyance, which I think only I noticed.

Later, I went to look at these two statues closely. They both had deep black gloss faces with fine features, thin

[1]Thank you, Hussein.

noses and small lips, and both had little pointy beards and wore white turbans. The beard and the turban made me think they were probably Arab Africans, like Hussein. I smiled to think of Hussein sitting in that grand house. He'd have loved it. He really enjoyed a big house and it was Georgian, his favoured architectural style. **You could have asked for a plus one and brought me along.**

I suspected the sculptures were a cack-handed attempt to convey the exoticism of foreign people to the citizens of colonial Britain who never ventured into the Empire. People wanted to own these sorts of artefacts to show they had connection with the money machine that the Empire became. Which, as Hussein had banged into my head, was no more than a huge looting operation **on-going looting operation with China joining in.** The statues weren't overtly insulting images, but I could see they were a problem. They were without identities, except a generic one: black Arab Muslim. Whereas the statues of white men placed in the alcoves as you ascended the staircase were not generic. They were of particular men and even had their names carved into the marble.

You didn't have to wander for too long in the Louvre, The Prado or the National Gallery to notice that white people had always basically refused to paint black people except in very narrow roles. In the modern era it changed, but glacially, and usually half-heartedly.

The earliest powerful images of a black person I came across when I looked for them, and which are still my favourite, are of Emperor Haile Selassie I. Ethiopian – of course. And haughty, a bit like our friend Hussein, and demanding of respect. Proud, strong and unbeaten, even though he did eventually lose control of his country and fled overseas. (A bit like our friend Hussein). Selassie's portraits tell a story of defiance and victory. He lost his country but never his dignity. There was one photo of him with a pair of panthers and another with a lion. Countless more existed of him wearing a rich variety of crowns, the most important one of which featured Selassie sitting on his imperial throne while Queen Elizabeth II and a man, who looked from the back like Prince Philip, bowed down to him. Christ, that must have hurt Philip. I have always believed that the images of the Emperor which somehow reached Jamaica gave comfort and hope to the people on that island, and were one of the foundation stones of the incomparable Rastafarian religion. The images of Marcus Garvey, another great, brave and brilliant politician who white people have no idea about, were numerous but not as strong, I suspected because he was caught up in the white gaze too entirely. He dressed not in Selassie's gilded cloaks and golden crowns, but as an English businessman, though Garvey did possess an impressive collection of hats with feathers in them, and, I have no idea why, a military uniform, though he was not in any army. Visually, Garvey seemed like he was always trying a bit too hard, unlike the crystal cool Selassie who was a natural style icon. Garvey was by far the better politician, philosopher and freedom fighter, but he didn't quite have the Emperor's personal style, which counts for a lot in Jamaica, and maybe the world, nowadays. Garvey had the lyrics: *Do not remove the kinks from your hair, remove them from your brain,* and *Up you mighty race, accomplish what you will!* but Selassie had the legs.

While I was at the bottom of the stairs, looking closely at the statues, I felt someone behind me. It was Trina

'I think it's time to move these two things,' I said. 'Come on.'

'Really?' she said. 'Okay. Where are we going to put them? Not in the lake?'

'No, they're not ours to do that with,' I said. 'Let's just place them over there in the corner, turn them to the wall and cover them in a bit of fabric.'

I lifted one, she the other, and we repositioned them. He was heavier than I thought. There's a surprise. He was freighting 400 years of shame and guilt and anger.

In the saloon, the other guests were looking at old photo albums which the owner of the house had left on the side board so people could admire his smart holidays and aristocratic mates. Skiing in winter, Scotland in summer. Princess Margaret. The Aga Khan. On one page a man held a rifle while standing beside a dead rhino whose two horns I recognised from above the kitchenette door where they were now mounted on a polished wooden board. Attached to the far wall of the chequered hall were a pair of ten-foot elephant tusks which turned up attached to their recently deceased owner on another page of the photograph album.

I didn't want to be in the saloon. I was happier at the bottom of the stairs. But I liked the people in the saloon. I had grown up with some of them. They were all amusing, clever, good people. But I was letting go of my old tribe. Joining a new one. Or was I making a new one by mixing the two rooms?

Later that evening, sipping cocktails before dinner and taking in the exquisite eighteenth-century landscape of dotted oaks, cute bridges and ornamental lakes, feeling like the inheritors of the earth, I noticed to my great joy (which I hid) that planted next to this extremely grand house were three of the species of trees which Ray had told me had slavery associations. What an opportunity!

'Do you see those trees there?' I opened with. 'They are not indigenous to Britain. I know this because I have a huge one in front of my house…' I felt the attention of the witty and impatient group loosening, but I knew I was about to draw it back in with my next sentence. 'They were planted to advertise an association with the slave trade.'

I thought I heard audible gasps of admiration, at least from one half of my crowd. The others, no doubt, thought *when will Guy stop banging on about slavery? It's so tasteless.* But I was no longer worrying about them. I was in the other tribe.

David said, 'Like pampas grass denotes a house full of swingers?'

'Quite like that,' I said.

As I looked up at the sky through the lacey canopy, my voice caught in my throat as I explained how the tree had come from Africa. There were a few of the others standing around listening to me, and I sensed I had gone on a bit too long on this rather depressing subject. But the rather depressing activity of slavery had gone on rather too long too, and until all these things were addressed and talked about it would continue to go on.

I felt that evening I had fully changed tribes, or at least left my old tribe contentedly leafing through vintage photograph albums in the saloon while I walked on. I silently thanked my neighbour Ray for putting the facts in my hand, so I could pass them on to my fellow citizens and friends. I was now a beacon of truth on the matter of Britain's racial history.

# 21.

After lecturing the powerful black people about my tree I returned home, flushed with success, and decided to check my facts. The tree was a Robina Pseudoacacia. I was relieved to discover that it was not indigenous to Britain. It had arrived here around 1640. So far so good. Its common names were False Acacia and Black Locust. It must be African with a name like that: Black Locust. And, er, what was black doing in the description? I quickly Googled black locusts. No such animal exists. We were now even segregating insects. I had the hardwood banged to rights. Things were falling in line for the slave trade connection, and the tree, I am afraid, no, I am proud to say, was for the chop. It was a good, tough wood compared to teak, according to the Internet, so it would burn well. As I chucked it on my fire on chilly, winter nights, it would warm both my body and my conscience. But try as I could, I could not actually find a mention of the association it had with the transatlantic slave trade on the Internet. I did discover that the False Acacia was not African. My heart sank as I thought about the lecture I had delivered to the VIP magazine editor and assembled house party guests. What would they say when they found I out I was spouting bullshit?[1] The tree was American. So that made the theory somewhat thinner. I Googled the hell out of it and found some celebrity False Acacias, which I was confident I'd turn up, as the Internet thrusts fame on anything, even a tree. There were two famous groves of Black Locust. One at Mount Vernon, and one at Monticello.

You may not immediately recognise those addresses. They were the country estates of two American Presidents: The first, and the third. George Washington and Thomas Jefferson (who also was the lead writer on the Constitution.) These were the white people who laid the foundation for America, whose values defined what America meant and who Americans were. They wrote the tablets of stone, and were the original moral arbiters. They were the ones who held the truths to be self-evident that all men are created equal while, at the same time, owning slaves who they worked to their deaths for profit.

And outside their handsome American homes grew groves of Black Locust. You can buy Black Locust saplings grown at Mount Vernon. The blossom produces especially sweet honey, but the whole thing left a bitter taste in my mouth.

[1]Both tribes would now want to expel me.

# 22.

Hussein and I had so little of the walk left to complete, and we finally took on the last pitch, a distance of seven miles, from Telford's aqueduct to my friend's house in its hidden valley. I went to pick up Hussein in Denbigh. Of course I did. I was his chauffeur. There was never any question of him having to use public transport. He had a phobia, okay, although not about trains, I suspected, but about mingling with the common people. As I drove, I remembered one occasion when I had driven a long way to pick him up in Denbigh and then motored back to Somerset, a journey that usually took five hours. Hussein said he wanted to go the scenic route via Leominster, so persuaded me to take the country roads rather than the M5. The trip took nearly seven hours and Hussein slept through most of it. **No need to worry when you have complete faith in the chauffeur.** I remember him coming back to the car from a tiny backwater garage somewhere in Shropshire with a sandwich, saying, 'I bought tuna. It was the only option available.' As though a smorgasbord of cold cuts and crudité should be laid out in front of the young prince whenever he decided to stop for refreshment.

By then I had grown to love his grand ways, to see him as the descendant of the Emperor. Down on his luck, maybe, but proud and picky. And every time I saw a black youth on city streets, particularly ones who looked skint and vulnerable, I delighted in thinking, *there goes a prince, or a lord, of a distant land.*

I was looking forward to the last stretch of our walk because I so wanted to get the bloody thing over with. Then I could write this book and get it out to the people, for better or for worse. We were on the final push, making our strike for the summit. I was also particularly keen to test drive the new post-Black Lives Matter UK environment with Hussein. Would the white people who I had heard responding to events on the radio, in print, on social media and TV actually behave differently when faced with Hussein (and me in the background)? Or was BLM, to white people, mainly bullshit?

As I was conducting an experiment about race, for a control, I went alone to the Glastonbury Tor and observed some walkers on my own. Everything was exactly as it ever was until I happened to see, ahead of me going up the hill, a mixed-race couple in their thirties. I actually heard them before I saw them, by listening to all the standard, white, walking folk passing them on their way down saying, 'Hello!' and 'Morning!' and, 'Phew, it's steep,' and, 'not far to the top!'

As we all reached the top and stood in the racing breeze to admire the patchwork quilt around us, I watched how many smiles and even little waves were aimed at this couple. Fancying myself a bit of a field expert in the study of BAME in the British countryside, I convinced myself there was a change.

Over the next couple of days, in Somerset at least, I became certain of an adjustment to the visible relations between the races. It coincided with the easing of the lockdown, with little foreign travel permitted, so I do not know if that skewed the data, but I was under the impression that there were many more BAME visitors around, and that white people were apparently out in packs hunting these people down and then being really polite to them. I stood for half an hour by a busy kissing gate to observe the phenomena, and I was sure it was real. I couldn't wait to try it out live with Hussein.

I turned up at the Denbigh house and heard, 'Grandpa!' shouted by the toddler rioters as they mobbed me. Inside, Hussein was still upstairs in his private suite while the women wrangled the kids.

'Mister Guy, what can I get you to eat, or to drink?'

'Nothing, I'm fine.'

'No no no, come on, sit down,' the chair was pulled out and on the table in front of me was placed a receptacle with nuts, seeds, dried fruits, pastries and homemade biscuits, soon followed by a short, dark, gritty coffee smelling of cardamom and acting like a line of coke. While I ate, the children crowded round me trying to catch my attention.

One clambered onto the bench and then over the gap onto my lap. My grandson put his warm, podgy, brown hand in my cold, mottled, white palm. I stared at our two hands until tears began to well up in my eyes. The women were still trying to fatten me.

'Samosa? I can make them very fast.[1] No trouble. Chicken and rice?'

[1] Make samosas? I thought you only ever bought them at a garage.

201

'No thank you, I am fine.'

And I was fine. Really fine, feeling the soft children pressing on me, chattering their heads off, 'Grandpa, look! Grandpa watch this!' I smiled at all that gave me joy right then: The open family. Integration. Acceptance. My African/English grandson at a Welsh-speaking school. How cool was that? I had learnt to appreciate all these things and many more from these people, little and big. Hybrid couples created not just better children but better parents, and better grandparents, and even a better nation. This was the room I wanted to be in.

In another room, Hussein was at his ease watching *How the West Was Won*, an epic movie about America pioneers. I went through to hurry him up and watched it for a bit and thought how so many simply embarrassing things – like a movie about the American genocide of the Indians – looked positively offensive with Hussein beside me. Not that he was offended. He laughed when I pointed out that the American rednecks had just invaded one country after another ever since the era of the movie.

I noticed a second TV with a broken screen turned against the wall.

'What happened to that?'

'The A-Rab threw a bottle at his brother and he ducked and it smashed the screen.' Hussein liked saying A-Rab in front of me.

In the kitchen, Hussein gave his last orders to the women. 'Take her off the table,' he pointed to a toddler who was crawling towards the sugar bowl, and he was then ready to be taken off by his driver. He was gang leader, I was soldier driver.

I gave Hussein a few quid as agreed, to cover some expenses on the walk, and I saw him give it to his mother.

202

When we got outside, I said, 'Don't give the cash to your mum. Keep it for when you're out and about.'

'No. It goes in the pot.'

'What if you need to get something? Or take a woman out for a coffee or whatever it is you guys do. In fact, what do Muslims do on a date? Most of the things I do are banned.' **Depends on the Muslim.**

'If I need to buy anything, I just ask Mum.'

That was the corollary of all the kids running towards you—if you shared the love, you shared the bills.

I waved goodbye to the mini mob.

I had written on Facebook a few days before that if you, as a white person, didn't have any black or brown people in your family, using a loose definition of the world family, then there was something wrong. Hussein asked me if I had meant it. I said I did.

'In 2020,' I said, 'in the United Kingdom, and indeed many other places, the absence of any brown or black people in your family after all this time looks to me like you've been avoiding them,' I said.

Hussein said, 'Guy, that's not right. There's not enough of us to go round. If you live outside the big cities, you'll find it hard to find a black or brown person — we only make up about 12% of the population.'

The beautiful phenomenon of mixed-race children is an irresistible tide lapping at the plywood bungalows of the white separatists. That's why the racists are so angry; they are being cornered by the rising number of people who they have designated the enemy.

I put the car in reverse, and went through my post BLM mantra: Act with openness and integrity at all times. Be cool. Trust black people. But do not be scared to say what you think.

We first decided to go and check out a couple of tourist attractions in Denbigh that Hussein had mentioned as interesting.

Our first stop was the ruined castle on the top of the hill above the town. The moment I saw it, I knew what was coming.

'Have you ever heard of Edward the First, Guy?' Hussein asked.

For those readers who don't know, Edward I was an English king who built a number of castles in the Welsh borders from which he brutally subjugated the Welsh. Although the ruined building I was staring at with Hussein looked like a castle out of a Robin Hood movie, featuring a merry hall for feasting and frolicking, it was basically built as a patrol post for the English army. It was a terrifying place where the English tortured Welsh men, women and children before chucking their corpses over the battlements into the moat.

'All that was a very long time ago,' I said.

'Thirteen hundreds. I read it on the board,' he pointed to an information board. 'You can tell the Welsh wrote it,' he chuckled. 'The English don't come out of it well.' Annoyingly, I found it hard to laugh. For some incredible reason I seemed to possess a residue of loyalty to Edward Longshanks, who was unquestionably a vicious dictator and, furthermore, had died 700 years before I was born. But it was deep inside me. In a dungeon, guarded by something scary.

There were actually two information boards on the grass in front of the castle—a bland one about the structure of the building, and a second, smaller one, tucked a bit out of the way, which dealt with the politics. It was to this one that Hussein led me. Its first paragraph read:

*The English settlers who founded Denbigh in the late thirteenth-century were outsiders planted here by their king intent on control. Their little town was contained within strong walls, while the oppressed and resentful Welsh were kept outside.*

Hussein crossed his arms and leant back a touch, clearly enjoying my discomfort.

'They could easily put similar notices on other statues and estates to show the full history,' he said. 'So for Churchill you'd have up his usual WW2 stuff and then put that he was also in charge when the Brits built concentration camps in Kenya after WW2 and had policies that led to millions of deaths in Asia. But I'm guessing most people would be against that, because as soon as that notice went up most sane people would question why we have a statue up of such a man.'

'Have you gone over to the Welsh?' I said.

'I live in Wales now,' he said. 'It's better than England.'

'But you don't have to take their side against the English,' I said.

'You weren't very nice to them, you know that?' He said, barely hiding his glee.

'We had our issues,' I said. 'I'm sure it took two.'

'I don't think so, Guy,' Hussein said. 'I think you stole their land and their money.'

'I wouldn't know about that,' I said, going back to the car. I started the engine and waited for Hussein to get in so I could get away from the place.

'There's a bit of a pattern emerging, I think,' Hussein said, getting in. 'With you English.'

'I thought I'd be safe here,' I said.

'Drive down there,' Hussein pointed. After a wiggle through the tight one-way system in the narrow streets he said, 'Pull over for a moment.'

I stopped the car outside the Denbigh town library, in front of a life-sized bronze statue of a man in nineteenth century clothing holding a pith helmet in one hand and putting out his other as if to greet someone with a handshake.

'Do you know who that is?' Hussein said.

'No,' I said.

'Sir Henry Stanley. Have you heard of him?'

'Yes,' I said. 'Did he come from Denbigh?'

'Yes. They say Stanley explored the Congo for King Leopold of Belgium. Have you heard of him?'

'Yes,' I said, miserably.

'It's a funny person to have a statue of,' said Hussein.

'It is,' I agreed.

I got out to look closer. A wag or maybe a BLM activist had attached a tiny white plasticine penis which peeped out of Stanley's flies. The statue was called *The Handshake - Dr Livingstone, I presume.*

It commemorated the moment two white guys met in Africa. Toe curling, really, when seen in the company of Hussein. A bit like watching *How the West Was Won* with him, but considerably worse.

I cringed more tightly when I read the inscription: Sir Henry Morton Stanley (1841–1904) Africa's greatest explorer.

The fact that his hand was outstretched to greet not one of the millions of Africans who lived on the continent (of which he was the greatest explorer) but for another white guy, David Livingstone (family motto: Christianity, Commerce and Civilisation) was not just embarrassing, it was also ludicrously impractical. Livingstone came from Lanarkshire, only a few days' exploring from Denbigh (unless it was me and Hussein walking and then leave two years), so the two great men could have saved themselves, and I suspect quite a lot of others, particularly Africans, a deal of trouble meeting somewhere like Manchester. Then I saw the date of the statue: 2011. An absolutely shocking time to be casting this image in bronze and placing it in the middle of a town. Or do I say that with hindsight? I hope not. Hussein mentioned that there was a lively campaign to get Stanley removed, but the vote to remove it failed. Hussein said, with more amusement than anger, that a woman he knew who lived in his street voted to keep it.

The statue was unveiled by a writer called Tim Jeale, poor, poor man. He was given the honour because he wrote a book called *Stanley: The life of Africa's Greatest Explorer*. I imagined the author and artist in 2011 together at the unveiling. I Googled the photos from the *Liverpool Post*.

I looked closely at a photograph from the newspaper of the mayor and two other pasty, white officials showing Stanley to five black people. They were a group of one woman and four men, all dressed with a colourful, African twist. Were they a delegation from the Congolese embassy on a jolly? All putting the past behind them with a photo op of *The Handshake*. Everyone was smiling. I wondered what they were thinking. You could stare at that photograph for a long time. The local councillors beamed. Even Stanley looked upbeat, despite the pigeon poo running down his left ear, though his tiny white penis was not yet attached, reaching out to shake the hand of the woman in the bright print dress for the cameraman. It was like a Jewish person being made to shake the hand of a statue of Goebbels to make Germans feel okay.

It was a massive miscalculation by the council, the artist and I think the biographer. Either on that day or between then and now they must have put their heads in their hands and wondered *what the hell was I thinking?* But I don't condemn them. Who am I to point that finger? I sympathised with their plight. They were caught on the wrong side of history. They shouldn't be made to stay there to be vilified, they should be allowed to cross back, however gingerly, to the right side. It is soon to become quite a well-worn track for white artists and writers to tread.

As Hussein said, considering Stanley claimed Congo for King Leopold of Belgium, one of the world's few megacides, i.e. personally responsible for the deaths of a million people (all African, in his case), *explorer* is not the word that now springs to mind. *Destroyer or Betrayer* may strike a more accurate note.

When, four hours later, I parked by the canal lagoon at the end of the aqueduct, where our final walk was to start, I sat in the front as Hussein grabbed his coat, boots and bottle and I thought, in full cliché mode, *ah, all that I have seen and all that I have learnt, this is the journey, this is the walk I have been on with Hussein.*

# 22.

[1]Guy said, 'Great, now we can start, my back's hurting a bit but once we get going, I'll feel fine.' He walked to the boot of the car and took out his boots. As he started putting them on, he struggled with tying his shoelace. I thought about offering to help, but thought it would sound a bit patronising and also thought if he can't tie his shoelaces then we're definitely not finishing the last 6 or 7 miles.

'What was Idris Elba's wife like?' Hussein said.[2]

We were walking away from the car towards a hand operated drawbridge over the canal, which was busy with pleasure boats and families enjoying barging holidays.

First thing I noticed was the street light that was still on at 11am in the morning on a sunny day, but Guy first noticed the disabled lift leading up to a house, 'My tax money being put to good use,' he said.

I said, 'You won't need that', for yes, Hussein had decided to wear the coke-dealer's knee length quilt coat,

---

[1]Go on, Hussein, you take up the story for the reader. Let's hear your words.
[2]I'm going to keep it moving along.

designed for a New York winter, on this humid, Welsh summer's day. Hussein's coat was like an overweight, hot and sweating member of our rambling party, always making us stop while it was moved from arm to waist to shoulder. The day quickly grew even hotter and I suggested we leave it in a hedge and return in the car the next day to pick it up, but Hussein baulked at that. I told him that apart from a sagging garbage bag of rotting rubbish I could not think of an item less likely to be stolen, but he clung on to it loyally.

I had mentioned to Hussein I had had dinner with Idris Elba and his partner when I was staying with my friends the Cotswolds.

'His wife was tall and beautiful,' I said.

'She's Somali,' Hussein said. 'Nice ass. East Africa makes the best women. Scientific fact. It's the most diverse place on earth genetically. Plus, it's where man came from. It's the centre of the world. That's why it makes beautiful people. Arabs, Chinese, Portuguese, Persians and I'm guessing Egyptians, Romans and Greeks all add to Somali blood.' **A major trade route for all things.**

'Any English in there?' I asked

'You add nothing to the flavour,' he replied. 'The English were too snobbish about mixing, luckily,' Hussein told me. 'The Egyptians actually called Somalia God's land. So of course the women are heavenly. Obviously. Standard.' **They called the Horn of Africa Ta Netjeru which apparently translates to God's land.**

'I thought she might be Somali from her looks.' I said. 'I was going to go and say hello to her.'

'You should have told her you have Somali family.'

'I was scared to,' I said.

210

'What? Why?' Hussein asked.

'I can't walk up to a black person and say Are you from Somalia? It's like saying I know you're not from here.'

'Oh, right,' said Hussein.

'It's sensitive,' I said.

We made our way down the towpath, enjoying the muted holiday atmosphere. The tourists had all emerged timidly from their Covid caves to blink at the sun, sniff the air for the first time in months, and see what the outside world was like. After all that time staring at four walls, it appeared it was bloody wonderful. Apart from my back, which was still hurting despite weeks of rest in lockdown, the world could not have looked livelier and more enticing. It was high summer, and a hot, rich day, the air thick with butterflies, dragonflies, bugs and floating willow seed.

I was proud to be out walking with Hussein, for many reasons: we were completing our mission, we were now firm friends, and I enjoyed his company, but also, since the BLM uprising, I felt what better man to be out in the countryside with?

We watched a middle-aged bloke, wiry with a white holiday stubble, jump off his slow moving barge and run ahead to raise the footbridge with the handle, leaving his wife to steer the boat through.

**I thought why would anyone want to live that life? Spend a bit of money to live in a tin that's about 2 metres wide?**[3]

As the barge slid by, I noticed the man eyeing Hussein and me. I puffed out my chest and may have put my arm

---

[3]Brimming with joy, isn't he?

around Hussein's shoulders. In a BLM world he was my bloody mascot. We exchanged a few words with the man. I sensed he disliked my patriarchal accent, but was confused, because he approved of Hussein. The glance he gave me said: *I can't get you on the race issue but I'm going to go with the catamite slur.*

Twenty minutes later, nearing the aqueduct we had been turned back on months before, we received a totally unsolicited and unprecedented, 'Hello! Afternoon!' from a short, bored man sitting in a picnic chair.

'Did you smile at him before he said afternoon?' I said.

'No,' said Hussein.

'Nor did I. Very interesting, eh?'

'Not really,' Hussein said.

'Keep a sharp eye out for more,' I said.

We walked past a family sat by a bench, exchanged hellos. Walked past three more groups, each said hi.

Guy said, 'interesting'.

I asked him, 'what's interesting?'

'I have just been wondering if our experience will change since BLM and I think it has, everyone's eager to say hello to us and especially you. You don't think so?'

I quickly replied with a 'nope'.

I thought Guy was looking into it too much, so explained to him I think it's the Covid effect rather than BLM, and that we'd all been locked in for the last four months with no outside contact so obviously everyone's jumping at every opportunity for human interaction. Guy was convinced BLM has had way more of an impact than I was.

We came to this aqueduct that Guy never stopped praising as a feat of British engineering, and I guess I agree it's an impressive structure, a bridge that boats cross and joins the two canals together. But whenever Guy gets going on his British did this and that marathon I see it as an opportunity to wind him up a bit for light entertainment.

'So how old is this aqueduct?' I asked Guy.

He said, 'Erm, Victorian so late 18th century or early 19th century?'

I don't need to say any more then.

On the other side we left the canal and cut across a field towards the steep hills to the north. We opened the map and both looked at it. Hussein found the page and I scanned the landscape in a well-practised combination that I would miss when the walk was over.

I said, 'Hopefully we are going to go right, here.'

We looked back at the map and said in unison, 'Yes', before glancing at each other and smiling. We plodded up the hill in single file towards the moorland. When we paused to catch our breath, we smiled to see how many extra miles of view we had earned since the last stop. Once or twice the troublesome nerve between two of my vertebrae emitted its shriek of pain, and I had to proceed bent over to my right, but I knew that our destination and the end of our journey was only five or so miles of torture away. It was the house of an old friend which stood a few yards from the Offa's Dyke Path. That's why it had been picked. We weren't heading to the summit of a mountain or the edge of a land mass. It was a pretty arbitrary destination, except that we had always said that THAT house was where we would stop. It was a promise we had made and a promise I was going to keep. There were too many broken promises between races. I was not going to throw this one on history's heap. So, onwards, and every time my left boot lost its footing I got 600 amps up my leg. But that would not stop me.

'Do you ever wonder,' Hussein asked, 'how the English took over the world? Stupid and lazy as you are?'

'I'll be honest,' I replied. 'It does sometimes confound me.'

We walked on in silence, past the back of the houses on the hillside, looking over the trampolines and bird tables into the lives of the inhabitants, and then trudged upwards, through shoulder high bracken where in places the path had been narrowed to a few inches by the lockdown. Paths needed people to exist. Buzzards wheeled and screeched high above us.

Hussein was on top form, striding metronomically into the lead, while at the same time maintaining a good line in historic grievances. It went from the return of African objects from that 'monument to looting' aka The British Museum, to why an Ethiopian religious relic called a tabot was kept in secret in Westminster Abbey, where Ethiopian priests were banned from viewing it.

'Only your high priest can see it, bro!' he shouted.

'Our high priest is called The Archbishop of Canterbury.'

'Yeah, well he's stopped the orthodox Ethiopian high priests from seeing it. Why would he do that?'

'Probably just doesn't like the smell of dope.'

We walked beside a long, mossy dry-stone wall and finally emerged onto a barren moorland striated with limestone outcrops. The path had taken us back to prehistory: to cavemen, to stone circles, to the ancient pagans.

'Can we stop?' I said, quickly thinking of something else to say to prevent him moving on. 'Cave dwellers would have lived up here. There are lots of burial mounds and stone circles,' I waved my arm around. It smelled of bracken and fern and sounded of lark song and the baaing of ewes and lambs. When we set off again, our feet pounded on hollow turf.

'You can imagine early man dressed in buffalo skins hunting animals up here,' I said.

'Yeah,' said Hussein, 'like mammoffs.'

We approached a fire spot burnt onto the turf.

'He walked on this very ground,' I said. 'Can we stop again? Thanks.'

Looking into the ash Hussein fell silent.

**My first thought was, it's nice that kids are getting out and about in the country, but Guy pointed out the littering.**

'It seems early man drank Peroni and ate maccy Ds,' I said.

A raven eyed us from a tranche of layered limestone and then took off a few feet to hover motionless on the wind.

As we passed walkers coming in the other direction we got a hello here, an acknowledgement there, and a smile in every face.

We sat down beside the road to rest my back again and received a full on wave from one passing car, and the next person – a lady with a grey bouffant – actually wound down her window, waved her arm and shouted, 'You won't get a bus there!' trying to have a joke with us. But suddenly, realising she may have in her excitement said the wrong thing (we've all been there) she called back, 'If you get lost just put your hand out.'

As they drove on I saw how wide her smile was. She had literally reached out to Hussein, and been kind and fun, and she had enjoyed it. **Reached out to both of us.**

215

These micro-affections didn't impress Hussein. He insisted they were nothing to do with the recent bollocking all white people had received under the guidance of BLM. I guess (he will no doubt tell me if I am wrong) he was thinking *I don't believe white people can suddenly make that shift.* **Yeah, you are wrong, that's exactly what I was thinking.**

I crabbed along the path behind Hussein under pale grey cliffs, where we heard, and then saw, four or five guys rock climbing high above us on the vertical pitches. You could just catch their conversation and the clicking of their equipment. They were young white men having fun, adding a bit of risk and danger to their lives which were otherwise too safe. I thought, *who's going to say it?* Then I did.

'White people shit.'

With a sheet of shale above us and a green valley below we weaved between megalithic rocks on the path. My body and my mind were in bad shape, and I jumped when a big black Labrador appeared out of nowhere and rushed us, barking with bared teeth.

'Woah!' Hussein shouted, 'black labs matter, bro!'

I burst out laughing and the dog stopped in its tracks and watched us walk by.

Half an hour later I gasped, 'Are we nearly there? How far can it be?'

We sat on a boulder, me so twisted I almost had my bum on the stone, my knee on the ground and my elbow on Hussein's shoulder. We looked at the map.

'It's less than two centimetres, Guy, you can do it. Give me your hand. Let me help you up.'

'We're nearly finished,' I croaked. 'Can you believe it?'

Hussein got me to my feet and walked on ahead. I was now more familiar with the back of that coat than his face.

'So, my friend, my comrade,' I called, 'my compatriot and fellow Englishman, as we draw near the end, tell me, has the journey been illuminating?'

'Yeah, quite. I must admit,' he said.

'Has it changed you at all? Given you new energy? Have you thought about going back out into the world and finishing your degree?'

I'm not sure he heard me, because he didn't answer. We were on slippery shale and with a steep drop to our left, both of us had to watch our footing,

'I hope I have made you think a bit,' I said. 'See things a new way,' I tried to sound upbeat. 'By the way, I've had a think about the credit for this book. I thought at first Guy Kennaway, with help from Hussein Sharif, or By Guy Kennaway. Edited by Hussein Sharif or Annotated by Hussein Sharif. But then I thought, no, it better be by Guy Kennaway and Hussein Sharif.'

'Okay.'

'And as for how we share the money...' I said.

He glanced back.

'I did think a 75 - 25% split would be fair, as I have done most of the writing....'

'Okay,' he said.

'But then I thought, that's not really in the spirit of the project. Is it?'

He grunted and shrugged.

'You know?' I said. 'The white guy gets most of the profits from a joint project with the black guy. It's not right.'

'Yeah. And people might find out,' he helpfully pointed out.

'I can't think how,' I said under my breath. 'So, I have decided we should go halves. It's simplest.'

'How much money will we make?'

'Depends how many people buy the book. We've got a great publisher so there's no one to blame if it falls flat.'

Hussein stopped and turned to me. 'I should have been more amusing,' he said. 'More popular, like the Kardashians. Said more bling things and had gold tipped walking boots.'

'You did okay, my friend,' I said.

'So, I might get some money?'

'We might. We live in hope,' I said. 'It could give you a start getting you back to uni.'

'No, I've already decided what I'm spending mine on, Guy.'

'Oh yes? You are aware it might not stretch to a private yacht?'

'I don't need much. I'm going to Africa.'

'Not another holiday? Hussein! It's time for action, young man.'

'No, not on holiday. I'm going to quit this country, and live in Kenya. I'm going to migrate.'

'You're leaving Denbigh? You're turning your back on Britain?'

'Yeah. Exactly that, bro. If I can,' he nodded, paused, then turned away. 'I want to live in Africa,' he said out loud. 'I want to get out of this country. This walk, these conversations, man, they've made up my mind.'

'You're just saying that to wind me up. Are you just saying that?'

'No, I'm not just saying it. I mean it. If I get money from this book I will move to Kenya.'

'What about the kids? They'll be heartbroken. They'll really miss climbing all over you and hanging on your sleeves. You're their guru.'

'They'll be visiting, and I'm sure I'll be coming back and forth.'

I started thinking how I would miss him. I looked at his spindly legs and puffy anorak. I damn well would miss him, if he went to Africa. We were becoming friends.

I said, 'I want to sit down again.'

'Come on, we're nearly there.'

'No, no. I'm fine. I just want to sit down.' As soon as I had got myself uncomfortable, I said, 'I'm … I'm … I'm surprised. It's not how I thought it would end, this walk.' Or this book, I didn't say. 'I thought you'd enjoyed it. All in all.'

'I did, Guy. Thanks. I have learnt. You got me out the flat. One thing the walk has shown me was that peace and quiet are not that bad. I used to hate the countryside. It's not as boring as I thought.'

So that was basically the sum total of the change wrought to Hussein after two years and 45 miles of walking and conversing with me?

'You did your best, Guy,' Hussein said. I think my head was in my hands. 'But I feel like Britain and Europe are on the brink, with anti-immigration and Islamophobia on the rise, and I've always worried that a day would come when the Brits will wake up and say, all of you get out.'

'You think I'd allow that to happen? Hussein!'

'But it's not up to you, Guy. So, I thought why not pre-empt all of that and move to a place with familiar people, sunshine, a simpler life, a growing economy, and my anxiety down to one, or sometimes zero. I remember coming back from Mombasa earlier this year. The plane was flying into London, we went through the heavy dark clouds, leaving the sun behind, and that's how I felt, like I'd left the sun behind. Anyway, the plane landed and with it my anxiety threw up for the first time since leaving the UK, must have got to seven in immigration, waiting in that queue, but I managed to get home, and then the place felt so depressing, cold and crammed. The opportunities in Kenya and in Africa are huge, so I'm gonna go back now.'

'I take this as a personal failure, Hussein. I was trying to mentor you.'

'Honest to God you shouldn't take it as a personal failure,' he said. I think I felt his hand lightly patting my back.

I got myself into as much of an upright position as I could and started along the path, which went from shale onto tightly nibbled grass that ran right up to the rocks and around the trunks of the hawthorn trees.

I was on automatic, fighting the lump hammer and high voltage shocks. I could hardly recall any of the countryside when I looked at the map to jog my memory later. I was soaking up the disappointment of Hussein's plan. He wanted to leave the United Kingdom, despite being given the opportunity to make his life here. Despite all I had told him about the greatest country on the planet, he wanted to go to Kenya. He rated Kenya above Britain. No disrespect to Kenya, but I cannot have done my job to sell this place well. I took it as a personal failure, but maybe it was Britain's fault. I thought, Christ – we've blown it with the likes of Hussein, and as for BLM, it's just too little too late. We have well and truly mucked this up. The good people, the people who really need to take us forward, are deserting. **I have to go. It's your country, it's my life. I can't live properly here with the way it is. I wish it could be another way. I know how Guy was hoping for us to hug at the end and swear we would be eternal friends. We can be friends, but I have to leave.**

Suddenly I couldn't go on. Something clicked in my spine and my left leg wouldn't respond to orders. There was something too wrong. I couldn't use my note pad; I could barely find words.

Hussein, will you write the account to the end? I'm done in. I'm beaten and upset. Will you do it for us, my friend? You are, after all, on half the money. And I, in my turn, and in my place, will be your footnote, with pride.

**I kept noticing and pointing out that the streams had dried up despite all the rain we've been getting for the last couple of weeks. It was quiet. I shared my facts with Guy about why we're always having a water shortage in the summer and how it's completely the water companies' fault for selling all the reservoirs to developers.**[4] **Africa has a lot of water just sitting underground and they just don't have the tech to reach it.**

**Guy said he was very thirsty and needed a drink. He did not look good. He had stopped talking which was very unusual. He was bent over on one side and his face was very badly twisted.**

**Guy was chanting, "I need to lose weight" (under his breath).**[5] **But I thought it was too late for that. He was,**

---

[4]He was never happier than with a decent grievance.
[5]This is possible.

like, crippled and shuffling. It reminded me of the 'I do believe in fairies' scene from Peter Pan, as Guy tried to speak his weight-loss into existence.

We walked for another couple of hours, past King Arthur's castle. At this point, Guy's situation had gotten worse, his back was aching and he was thirsty. We got to a place where water usually runs down the mountain and Guy asked for my water bottle. I told him there's no more water, and passed him the bottle. Guy got onto his knees trying to get the remaining droplets coming off the mountain into the bottle. I actually felt sorry for him.

'Please God,' he said to the dry stream, and then bent to put his mouth on the ground to suck water. It was sad.

I helped him up and held his arm to get him moving again. The evening was getting dark, and the cloud was just over our heads in the cliffs. I thought *how am I going to get him off here if he breaks down?*

He said, 'You know we have to make it?'

We slowly got round the bend.

Then I heard my name and Guy's name being called from below, and saw the house in the bottom of the valley.

We made it, I said.[6]

---

[6]Thank you, Hussein. God's speed to you in Kenya. I shall be coming to do our Africa tour. This isn't over, my friend.

# A NOTE ON THE AUTHOR

**Guy Kennaway** was born in London in 1957. In all Kennaway's work he champions the underdog. He searches out communities under pressure, and tries to make the best of their troubles with tenderness and laughter. He is best known for *One People* about a Jamaican village threatened by mass US tourism, *Bird Brain* about a community of optimistic pheasants and *Time to Go*, the funniest book about assisted suicide ever. His latest novel, *The Accidental Collector*, is also published in 2021.

**Hussein Sharif** was born in Kenya in 1996. He came to Britain when he was 8, living in Tottenham, and attending the University of Kent 'for a bit'. *Foot Notes* is his first book.

'I like to float about; many things happen to me that shouldn't happen, and things turn out to be blessings in a weird kind of way. I love family, traditional food, and try to be a good Muslim, though often fail.'